T0340186

EQUIPMENT QUALIFICATION IN THE PHARMACEUTICAL INDUSTRY

Aspects of Pharmaceutical
Manufacturing Series

EQUIPMENT QUALIFICATION IN THE PHARMACEUTICAL INDUSTRY

STEVEN OSTROVE, PH.D.

Ostrove Associates, Inc.
Elizabeth, NJ, United States

ELSEVIER

ACADEMIC PRESS
An imprint of Elsevier

Academic Press is an imprint of Elsevier
125 London Wall, London EC2Y 5AS, United Kingdom
525 B Street, Suite 1650, San Diego, CA 92101, United States
50 Hampshire Street, 5th Floor, Cambridge, MA 02139, United States
The Boulevard, Langford Lane, Kidlington, Oxford OX5 1GB, United Kingdom

Notices
Knowledge and best practice in this field are constantly changing. As new research and experience
broaden our understanding, changes in research methods, professional practices, or medical
treatment may become necessary.

Practitioners and researchers must always rely on their own experience and knowledge in evaluating
and using any information, methods, compounds, or experiments described herein. In using such
information or methods they should be mindful of their own safety and the safety of others, including
parties for whom they have a professional responsibility.

To the fullest extent of the law, neither the Publisher nor the authors, contributors, or editors, assume
any liability for any injury and/or damage to persons or property as a matter of products liability,
negligence or otherwise, or from any use or operation of any methods, products, instructions, or ideas
contained in the material herein.

Library of Congress Cataloging-in-Publication Data
A catalog record for this book is available from the Library of Congress

British Library Cataloguing-in-Publication Data
A catalogue record for this book is available from the British Library

ISBN **978-0-12-817568-2**

For information on all Academic Press publications
visit our website at https://www.elsevier.com/books-and-journals

Publisher: Andre Gerhard Wolff
Acquisition Editor: Erin Hill-Parks
Editorial Project Manager: Sandra Harron
Production Project Manager:
Kiruthika Govindaraju
Cover Designer: Greg Harris

Typeset by SPi Global, India

Working together
to grow libraries in
developing countries

www.elsevier.com • www.bookaid.org

Dedication

I would like to dedicate this book to my family, to my wife Karen, who has stood by me through many years of my being on the road working at many pharmaceutical, biotech, and device plants and having to take care of everything. To my children Elliot, Philip, and Naomi who have withstood and understood my absence from home due to my travel, working at home (where I needed quiet), and much much more. To them, I owe a debt of gratitude for their caring and support.

In addition, I want to say thank you and acknowledge all the engineers, scientists, quality assurance personnel, and all those with whom I have met and worked with throughout my career.

Contents

Acknowledgments

In the preparation of this book, I have had the invaluable assistance from my good friends and colleagues Mr. Dave Maynard, Mr. Phil DeSantis, and Dr. Ken Blashka. Each one provided helpful comments on some or all of the chapters in order to make them better. I appreciate their assistance and knowledge of equipment qualification.

Introduction to aspects in pharmaceutical manufacturing

Welcome to a new series of books dealing with various "Aspects in Pharmaceutical Manufacturing." This series is intended to provide information to those just coming into the industry, guidance for those already working in the industry, and/or those who just want to "brush up" on their knowledge of the various specific aspects of pharmaceutical manufacturing. Each book in the series will be primarily designed to address the WHY and the HOW of specific pharmaceutical aspects, for example, equipment qualification, cleaning, and biotech—upstream and downstream operations.

Examples and references will be provided to help guide and support the information presented. The authors were all selected because of their expertise and their ability to present this knowledge in a clear and concise manner.

Although many of the topics to be covered in this series may been seen in other works and covered in general, each book in this series will cover one specific aspect of the manufacturing process or environment. Reasons behind and the methods needed to implement a compliant program for that aspect of pharmaceutical manufacturing will be explained.

Topics in this series can fill in the gaps in the education of pharmaceutical employees. Knowledge obtained in formal education settings often lacks in real world conditions such as emergencies that are often encountered in pharmaceutical or biotech manufacturing. The information provided to the reader will help stimulate formulating compliant solutions in GMP documentation, resolving problems (getting to the root cause), and more.

Each book could be used in classroom settings (pharmaceutical engineering) or by individuals interested in improving their subject knowledge (for advancement or other needs), which is important to improving industry compliance to current government regulations.

It is through continuous improvement from books like this one and others in the series that the industry and the individual will grow, improve, and lead to better, more effective, and safer pharmaceuticals.

Steven Ostrove, PhD

Introduction

There are several aspects to performing a good equipment qualification program. This book presents many of the ideas and possible solutions collected over many years in the industry.

As we begin the process of understanding how to perform an equipment qualification, several questions come to mind:

- Why do we need to qualify the equipment?
- Who can or who does the qualification?
- What needs to be qualified?
- What is qualification?
- How much is it going to cost?
- How long will it take?

In answer to the first question, qualification is needed for two major purposes. The first purpose is to demonstrate that the equipment is what was ordered and that it will function as needed for its intended use. In fact, if you think about it, everyone performs a qualification every time they purchase a new item: a new car, a new toaster, or a new house. The same steps are followed in determining that the unit is the one you want and that it works as you expect it to work. The big difference is that for the personal items the requirements and results are not being recorded. The second purpose is it is the law as specified in the Code of Federal Regulations (CFR) Title 21.[a]

In answer to the second question, qualification usually falls at least in part on the engineering group but can be done by the validation group or any other person or group that is qualified and knowledgeable on the use and operation of the equipment and that has the training and experience to perform the tasks required.[b]

In answer to the third question, read on. According to interpretation of the CFR Title 21,[c] all equipment used in the manufacturing of a pharmaceutical (Aseptic, OTC, Tablet, device, etc.) and all equipment used in the laboratory for in-process testing or release and/or any unit used for the

[a] Title 21 CFR §211.63, Food & Drug Administration, 2017
[b] Title 21 CFR §211.25
[c] 21 CFR Parts 211 and 820.

Equipment Qualification in the Pharmaceutical Industry
https://doi.org/10.1016/B978-0-12-817568-2.00001-4

production of a device (classes I–III) needs to be qualified to be sure that they will work as intended and that the results of the testing are accurate and true results.

As to the fourth through sixth questions, often asked by management, this depends on the scope of the project, that is, number of units to be qualified, and the expertise of those doing the qualification (i.e., time it takes to write and execute the protocols). In short, qualification demonstrates that the equipment meets the requirements of the users, was received on-site in working order (or fixable), and will function as the users expect it to work for their product. Expense is not a valid consideration in determining how the program will be performed since it is required by the Food and Drug Administration (FDA) to be able to sell your product in the United States. That is what this book is all about.

In answer to the fifth and sixth questions, it depends. It depends on the number and complexity of the equipment to be qualified. It depends on the experience of the qualification team. It depends on previous experience and availability of protocols for similar units. And it depends on the risk analysis for each unit as it pertains not only to production but also to patient safety.

To further our understanding of the qualification process, three basic terms need to be defined and understood prior to taking on a Food and Drug Administration (FDA) qualification project. These are the following:

- Compliance
- Qualification
- Validation

Compliance

According to the web dictionary[d]:
- "…the action or fact of complying with a wish or command"
- "… the state or fact of according with or meeting rules or standards"

Qualification

According to the web dictionary[e]:
- "a condition or standard that must be complied with"[f]

---

[d] www.Dictionary.com
[e] ibid.
[f] www.Merriam-webster.com

Validate/validation

According to the web dictionary[g,h]:

- to make legally
- to support or corroborate on a sound or authoritative basis
- to give legal force to; legalize
- to give official sanction, confirmation, or approval to, as elected officials, election procedures, documents, etc.

The obvious first reason heard for qualifying process equipment is because the Food and Drug Administration (FDA) of the United States requires all pharmaceutical companies who manufacture, hold, or distribute a drug product or substance (virtual or other) to be compliant with the rules set out in the Federal Food, Drug, and Cosmetic (FD&C) Act as promulgated in the Code of Federal Regulations (CFR). But, qualification is employed for another very important (business) reason: "Did you receive what you ordered, and does it work as you need it to work?" As in the opening paragraph, qualification is performed every time a new purchase is made:

> For example, you purchase a new toaster. First the box is inspected, intact, and not damaged. Then the unit is removed from the box and placed on the counter. Question, is it what you expected the unit to be? Does it have two slots or four? The unit is then plugged in, and a piece of bread is inserted into one of the slots. The toast level is set, and the bread plunger is depressed. When it pops out, you check it for the level of darkness you like. Repeat as necessary (commissioning) until it is correct.

This example just followed all of the qualification steps that will be followed in manufacturing except it was not written down.

To accomplish the state of compliance (meeting rules or standards, in this case the FDA's), companies need to have a program of qualification and one of validation. In the pharmaceutical industry, all qualification work needs to be completed following a written program. Industry standard currently uses the term qualification for all process equipment or utilities used in or supporting the manufacturing operation to say or demonstrate that they meet the conditions required to perform their job in the pharmaceutical process. The term validation or compliance applies to the demonstration of the successful testing of the entire process (i.e., the entire manufacturing

---

[g] ibid.
[h] www.Dictionary.com

process). Thus a company cannot achieve the "compliant" state without completing equipment qualification first and then process validation.[i]

Both equipment qualification and process validation follow similar procedures. As stated in Title 21 of the CFR Part 211 §63:

> Equipment used in the manufacturing, processing, packing, or holding of a drug product shall be of appropriate design, adequate size, and suitably located to facilitate operations for its intended use and for its cleaning and maintenance.

Note here that the FDA is not specific about what needs to be done. The equipment needs to be appropriately designed and of a size that accommodates the process, as well as cleanable and maintained. It is up to each company to decide how to "qualify" the equipment. That is, proving that the equipment meets its intended use, its design will make the product effectively without adding to or taking anything out of the product, and it can be cleaned (all components or ingredients or materials used in the manufacturing process can be removed to a provable safe level), and it can be effectively maintained.

The CFR does not specify or even hint at what to do. Qualification (meeting the standard established by the industry and the FDA) of the equipment is one part of reaching a compliant state. It is up to the individual company to determine how to qualify each piece of equipment or utility used to support the process.

This book will provide information on interpreting the requirements set forth in the CFR and explain how to meet current industry standards and expectations. This is Current Good Manufacturing Practice (CGMP). Please note the word current as it underscores current industry standards and practices in the manufacturing operation. It implies that current good engineering practices (GEP) and techniques and current industry standards are used in the equipment design and that current scientific thought is used to test and approve the function of each piece of equipment. In addition, the FDA has promulgated a guidance document that discusses not only the use of the equipment but also the risk associated with a failure.[j]

Some of the topics to be covered include the following:

- Computer control of equipment and where to include in the equipment qualification
- Cleaning considerations
- Requalification

---

[i] S. Ostrove, "How to Validate a Pharmaceutical Process", Elsevier, 2016.
[j] International Commission on Harmonization (ICH) Q9 and FDA Guideline for Risk Management

- Equipment design considerations
- Environmental conditions
- Commissioning and decommissioning
- Preparing the qualification protocol(s)

Chapter 9 will provide a matrix for some of the major types of equipment used in pharmaceutical manufacturing. The chapter is not meant to be an absolute requirement for the equipment listed, but a guide for consideration. Remember that the use, cleaning, risk, and maintenance must be carefully considered and evaluated prior to starting the qualification procedure.

Types of qualification

There are four recognized types of qualification today. The FDA prefers the "prospective" approach since the acceptance criteria are preplanned removing the possibility of "testing into compliance."

The four types are the following:

- Prospective—preplanned tests with preplanned results.
- Concurrent—same as prospective except, the unit can be used as it is being qualified.
- Retrospective—basing qualification on past history of the unit.
- Requalification—to be performed only when there is a change to the equipment (e.g., moving or other changes) or process or, as required to demonstrate continued compliance due to its function, for example, drying oven or autoclave.

As above the expected approach is the prospective one. It gives the highest assurance that the unit will function as intended and will reliably fulfill its intended function. To perform a prospective qualification program, one needs to first know what the user wants the equipment to do. From this a plan can be made to test the ability of the unit to perform those functions with known expected results.

The order of the qualification process

As can be seen in this introduction, the qualification of process equipment and even some of the utilities supporting the equipment can be quite complex. However, there is a basic order to completing the process successfully as shown in the succeeding text (Table 1).

Table 1 Order of the Qualification Program

- Need established
- Equipment type determined to meet needs
- Process engineers design process and specify needs
- Submit bids to vendors for each specific piece of equipment
- Vendor bid review
- Selection of vendor
- Factory Acceptance Test (FAT)
- Site Acceptance Test (SAT)
- Commissioning
  - Fix up (as necessary)
- Qualification
  - Installation qualification
  - Operational qualification
  - Performance qualification (as needed)
- Equipment in use
- Decommissioning
- Equipment removed from production line

One extra note of caution: writing, reviewing, and executing the qualification documents take time (see Chapter 6). Allow sufficient time for proper conduct of this part of the entire qualification program. It takes more time than originally planned—remember Murphy's rule. If it can go wrong, it will and at the worst time.

CHAPTER TWO

Getting ready: Documentation

Overview

Preparing for the process equipment qualification program is probably the most important step in the qualification program. It takes time, but it is well spent if done correctly. Management often feels that this part is easy and that the operators, qualification specialists, engineers, and others have knowledge of the equipment without further reading, understanding, and/or researching to be able to write and execute the qualification protocols without any further research. Here is an example of what I mean:

> A question was asked how I knew how to qualify all of the process equipment in their facility. While they had several items that were similar (e.g., tanks and blenders), each has a unique purpose in their operation. The answer I gave is really quite simple: "Before investigating I don't know the specific function of each one. But I do understand their implied function (blending components, holding liquids, etc.) the documentation supplied by the vendor, or operations staff, will tell me the rest."

But before any qualification activity takes place, a series of events need to occur, for example, designing the equipment to the specific function, ordering the equipment, and reviewing the bids form the vendors.

Please note that even with research, there needs to be a basic knowledge of the use of the equipment before preparing any qualification protocol (Chapter 8) or performing any commissioning (Chapter 7). As in my answer earlier, most people have this basic idea of the use of the equipment: blenders blend, granulators granulate, tanks hold liquid, etc. But we also need specific knowledge of the function of the unit that can be obtained from the process engineers and/or the operation group. The purchasing department then has to be informed (e.g., by process engineers, operations, and development) of the needs and requirements of the equipment to be ordered. The manufacturers purchasing group in turn needs to communicate their needs clearly to the vendors so that the vendor can produce a bid that meets the specific requirements. For example, when ordering an autoclave for sterilization as part of the process, one would need to be sure that there is a "validation port" and that it can have a pressure hold test. On the other hand, if the autoclave is just for "kill" purposes, then the validation port may not be needed.

The following is a short list (also see Fig. 1) of things that should be done in obtaining a new process unit:

- Operations discuss needs with process engineers.
- Process engineers' design determine the type, size, and other specific functions of the unit.
- Process engineers confirm all specifications with operations.
- If, and when, all are in agreement, the purchasing department requests bids from vendors.
- Vendor *bids are reviewed* (VERY IMPORTANT) by validation/engineering/operations for consistency with needs.
- Vendor is selected, and the order is placed (be sure to order sufficient number of manuals, for example, operation, cleaning, and maintenance at this time).

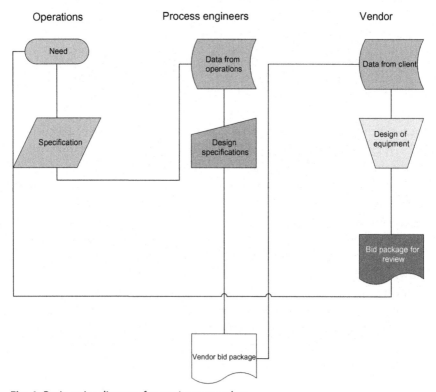

Fig. 1 Basic swim diagram for equipment orders.

Once the order is submitted to the vendor and the unit is ready to be sent to the site, some pretesting to assure that the unit works as the company needs is often performed (for large or expensive units). This is called the factory acceptance test (FAT). The manufacturer of the unit usually prepares the test protocol for this test, but it is very important that the operation company both witness and add some specific tests of their own to assure it will meet the requirements of the purchase order. Assuming all goes well with the FAT, the unit is ready to be shipped to the operation company. Upon receipt at the operations site, the site acceptance test (SAT) should then be performed followed by commissioning (see Chapter 7).

Documentation

Thus it is important to make sure that the qualification team has all of the necessary documentation for each unit and that the person assigned to prepare the commissioning protocol (Chapter 7) and the qualification protocol (Chapter 8) speaks to the users to understand the unit's specific function in the process.

As stated in the beginning of this chapter, obtaining and reviewing the documentation supplied by the operations group, the process engineers, and the vendor take time. This time is well spent and is needed to collect the relevant documents, to review the documents, and to be sure that they are fully understood. It should not be considered "wasted" time nor be thought of as unnecessary training. Regardless of the experience of the qualification person, time up front collecting and reviewing documents as well as talking with those who are involved in the process design or use will certainly pay off with a professional, well-prepared, and unquestioned protocol and thus a faster release of the unit to production and process validation.

The following is a general list of sources for the information required (Tables 1 and 2).

While the documentation obtained from the sources earlier is critical to a successful qualification, so is talking to the operators and the process development staff. Here are some examples of questions to ask (Table 3).

In preparing for a qualification program that includes commissioning and qualification and process validation, there are two main components.

Each of these requires their own unique set of documents or protocols. The commissioning protocol, as discussed further in Chapter 7, is needed to guide the commissioning process and prepare the equipment for qualification and thus use. The qualification protocols are prepared specifically for

Table 1 Usual documents needed for protocol preparation.

Document	Specific doc.	Comments
Drawings		
	PFD	
	P&ID	
	Vendor	
	Isometric	Only for WFI
Manuals		
	Operation	
	Cleaning	
	Maintenance	Regular and preventive
SOPs		
	Operation	
	Preventive maintenance	
	Cleaning	
	Emergencies	
	Backup	
	Training	
	Calibration	
Reports		
	Weld	Welder qualification, weld reports
	Pressure	
	Balance	HVAC
	Vendor	FAT/SAT
	Passivation	
	Calibration	
Specifications		
	User (URS)	
	Functional (FRS)	
	Engineering	
	Operating ranges	
Other		
	Standards	
	Ladder logic	
	Source code	
	Batch record	
	Instrument list	
	Line list	
	Contractor certifications	For example, welders

each unit system. This means that each is set into a protocol representing the process equipment as a stand-alone unit (e.g., a cold room or an autoclave).

Thus the unit can be used independently to achieve a given process function. For example, as in the preceding text, a refrigerator is a stand-alone

Table 2 Where some of the documents are to be used.

IQ/OQ/PQ	Item	Comments
IQ/OQ	Operations manual	
IQ/OQ	Cleaning manual	
IQ	Preventive maintenance manual	
IQ	P&ID (as built)	
IQ	PFD	
IQ	Purchase order	Referenced only
IQ/OQ/PQ	Current SOPs	See Chapter 6
IQ/OQ/PQ	User requirements	
IQ/OOQ/PQ	Design specifications	
IQ	LOGS (cleaning/use/maintenance)	
IQ/OQ	Calibration (last/next)	Include in OQ
IQ	Reports (e.g., weld)	
IQ	Equipment arrangement drawings	

Table 3 Some basic questions to be asked.

1. How critical is the equipment to the process?
2. Product contact: direct, indirect, none?
3. Is the unit part of or involved in a critical process parameter (CPP)?
4. Are the manuals available?
5. Are the P&IDs available?
6. Is there anything specific or unique about the process or operation of the equipment?
7. What speeds, temperatures, pressures, etc. are to be used?
8. Are there any safety issues for the equipment (e.g., solvents and acids/bases)?
   a. Safety concerns for the operators?
   b. Other safety concerns?

unit. It contains many key components that allow it to function as a unit. A pump, while able to operate on its own, does not constitute a stand-alone unit since a pump isolated from a tank or other vessels does nothing for the process. This is where the engineering drawing(s) come into play in preparing the documents. System boundaries need to be established before any writing can begin. This is why the piping and instrument drawing (P&ID), the process flow drawing (PFD), and the vendor drawings are so important. The collection of the correct documentation is critical to completing a successful qualification program (Table 4).

Table 4 Usual SOPs for the preparation of qualification documents.

- Writing a protocol
  - IQ
  - OQ
  - PQ
- Operation
- Emergency
- Change control
- Cleaning
- Maintenance
- Reviewing a protocol
- Execution a protocol
- Writing a qualification final report

Document specifics
Validation master plan

The validation master plan (VMP)[a] is a key document to guide the entire compliance program. The VMP presents the approach to the qualification and validation of the project. It provides guidance as to which process units require full qualification and which units require commissioning only (see Chapter 7 for commissioning). It provides basic information about the testing that is expected and the documents that support those tests.

In addition, the VMP will provide a list of expected standard operation procedures (SOPs) for each unit in the process and information on how the ancillary GMP programs will be incorporated and more.

Drawings

The engineers who designed the process will provide the drawings necessary to prepare the protocols. The drawings that are needed are the process flow drawing (PFD) and the piping and instrument drawing (P&ID). Other drawings from the engineering staff may also be required when the utilities are qualified. Drawings from the vendors will also be needed as verification as to what is actually built. Vendor drawings are needed when collecting documents so as to understand what components are contained, in what

---

[a] International Society for Pharmaceutical Engineering (ISPE) Baseline "Commissioning and Qualification" Vol. 5. Chapter 6, March 2001.

order, and each unit they is used and connected. Note that all of the drawings used will be verified during the protocol execution (also known as "walking the drawing or protocol").

The P&ID is needed so that the qualification personnel can set the "system boundaries" for each unit. This means that the P&ID is reviewed and marked (using colored markers) so as to indicate that all components (pipes, valves, pumps, etc.) are included, in a protocol, as needed so as to make the unit "stand-alone." In the P&ID, all components of the equipment are numbered for easy identification. The piping is also numbered as are the valves and all other major operational components (e.g., tanks, heat exchangers, controllers). These numbers are often used in the preparation of the protocol.

Manuals

One of the items that needs to be requested at the time of ordering a piece of process equipment is the associated manuals for that unit. At a minimum the operation, cleaning, and preventive maintenance manuals should be requested. In fact a copy should be requested for each of the following groups (NOTE: depending on the operation size, some groups may not need the equipment documentation):

- Operations
- Maintenance
- QA
- Qualification/validation
- Library/records

Requesting additional copies at a later date can prove to be very costly in both lost time and money spent.

SOPs

The first SOP that should be reviewed is "How to prepare a qualification protocol." There may be others specifically for preparing the installation qualification (IQ), the operational qualification (OQ), or the performance qualification (PQ). Other SOPs (e.g., how to execute a qualification protocol, good documentation practices, reviewing the executed protocol, and writing the final report) will probably be required to be reviewed so that the document preparation and protocol execution will meet corporate standards and FDA documentation requirements also (Table 4).

Thus the Code of Federal Regulations Title 21 (21 CFR) Part 211[b] and any other relevant FDA, International Council on Harmonization (ICH), or other guidelines should also be reviewed and consulted.[c]

The following rule of thumb should be considered when developing the SOPs. First the IQ protocol does not need any SOPs for its preparation or execution. The list of SOPs to be needed is to be found in the VMP or as a list in the IQ. For the OQ the SOPs should be available in draft form for execution so as to be used during the execution as needed, and changes can be made without going through the change control process. However, for the PQ, the SOPs need to be signed and effective.

Operations/vendors/others

Before beginning the planning of a qualification and validation program, all those assigned to preparing or executing the qualification protocols need to have a basic understanding of the process. As discussed the PFD is thus important as is a talking point between the process engineers, operators/users, vendors, etc. Look for previous protocols or documents for the equipment to be qualified. Look at the FDA warning letter site[d] for information about related FDA warning (forewarned is forearmed as the saying goes).

Summary

Collecting all the expected information takes time. It is worth the effort. Having the information available when the protocol is prepared saves time in errors, in writing the protocol, and in being sure all components are included. The P&IDs are needed to correctly determine system boundaries. Keep in mind that a single P&ID may contain one or more systems to be qualified. The PFD is useful in guiding the reader through the protocol, while not all the documentation listed in Table 1 is necessary to complete the protocol (most of it will be needed at some point).

---

[b] 21CFR211.63, and 21CFR211.65.
[c] International Commission on Harmonization, e.g., "ICH Q10, Pharmaceutical Quality System" May 9, 2007.
[d] http://www.FDA.gov.

Quality systems

The last chapter discussed the basics of the documentation generally needed for the preparation of a qualification protocol. This chapter goes further in its discussion of other aspects of the qualification program that need to be considered (usually before the qualification begins). There are other activities and documents that need to be considered, completed, and/or developed for the qualification program to be complete. These documents and programs are known as the companies' quality system programs and are an integral part of all qualifications. Some of these will have, or should have, been in place all along before the qualification; others such as the preventive maintenance program may still be a "work in progress" depending on the company's status (start-up or developed operation). The quality systems used in equipment qualification (a more complete list of quality systems is seen in Table 1) include but are not limited to the following:

- Risk management
- Change control
- Qualification investigations (different than production investigations)
- Corrective action (CAPA)
- Calibration/metrology
- Preventive maintenance
- Cleaning
- Document control
- Requalification

These systems are key to a successful qualification program. Others, as seen in Table 1, may also be important for your project. The quality system approach includes more than just ICH Q10[a]; it includes Q8[b] and Q9[c] and others.

---

[a] ICH HARMONISED TRIPARTITE GUIDELINE PHARMACEUTICAL QUALITY SYSTEM Q10.
[b] ICH HARMONISED TRIPARTITE GUIDELINE Pharmaceutical Development Q8.
[c] ICH QUALITY RISK MANAGEMENT Q9.

Equipment Qualification in the Pharmaceutical Industry
https://doi.org/10.1016/B978-0-12-817568-2.00003-8

Table 1 Other quality systems.

1. Training
2. Personnel
3. Qualification—equipment
4. Validation—process
5. Environmental auditing
6. Audits
   a. Internal
   b. External
7. Vendor qualifications
   a. Quality agreements
8. Documents
   a. Preparation
   b. Storage
   c. Recovery
   d. Document reviews (e.g., SOPs)
9. Pest control
10. Quality control laboratory
11. Technology transfer
12. Packaging (primary through shipping)
13. Labeling (control)
14. Warehousing
    a. Storage
    b. Shipping
15. Distribution
16. Complaints
17. Recalls
18. Stability
19. Investigations
    a. Lab OOS
    b. Qualification
    c. Production (OOS and others)

Quality risk management

Today, all qualification and validation processes should be based on good science and a risk-based approach[d,e] according to the FDA.[f] The risk management program itself should be based on a good scientific background. There are two aspects of risk analysis that can or should be

[d] Ibid.
[e] FDA GMPs for the 21st Century.
[f] PHARMACEUTICAL CGMPS FOR THE 21st CENTURY—A RISK-BASED APPROACH—FINAL REPORT.

considered. The first is risk to the patient, and the second is risk to production. The FDA's key interest is making sure there is no or at least very limited risk to the patient due to production issues (dose, packaging, distribution, etc.) or to the manufacturing process itself. This would include the loss of product due to equipment failure, thus leading to a possible shortage of the medication or device. The FDA states[g] that patient safety should always be the primary concern of all manufacturing.

Thus, this is every manufacturer's goal. An analysis needs to be made of each process step and therefore each process piece of equipment, with a determination of its criticality and its impact on the process.

One of the most common approaches to determining the risk of a unit is the use of the failure mode effect analysis or FMEA. An example of an FMEA can be found in Tables 2 and 3. There are several good references on how to set up and perform a FMEA.[h,i]

Table 2 Example of an FMEA.

Owner	Item		Detectability	Occurrence	Severity	Cause RPN
Engineering	Mixer					
		Runs slow	4	1	5	20
		Runs fast	4	1	5	20
		Intermittent fast and slow	2	2	5	20
		Product level low	5	3	5	75
		Product level high	4	3	5	60
		Power loss	5	1	1	5
Compounding	API					
		High trace metals	2	3	4	24
		Clumped	4	3	3	36
		Smell	5	1	2	10
		Combined lots	5	2	3	30
		Combined different suppliers	1	2	3	6
		Color incorrect	2	3	4	24
		Particle distribution low	3	4	5	60
		Particle distribution high	3	4	5	60
Operations	Batch record					
		Missing a page	4	2	5	40
		Not approved completely	4	1	5	20
		Old version	5	2	5	50

Detectability: 1 = easily detectible; 5 = not easily detectable.
Occurrence: 1 = not often; 5 = often.
Severity: 1 = not severe; 5 = very severe.

[g] ibid.
[h] FMEA—you-tube.
[i] FMEA for beginners—www.ASQ.org.

Table 3 FMEA sorted by RPN.

Owner	Item	Detectability	Occurrence	Severity	RPN
Engineering	Power loss	5	1	1	5
Compounding	Combined different suppliers	1	2	3	6
Compounding	Smell	5	1	2	10
Engineering	Runs slow	4	1	5	20
Engineering	Runs fast	4	1	5	20
Engineering	Intermittent fast and slow	2	2	5	20
Operations	Not approved completely	4	1	5	20
Compounding	High trace metals	2	3	4	24
Compounding	Color incorrect	2	3	4	24
Compounding	Combined lots	5	2	3	30
Compounding	Clumped	4	3	3	36
Operations	Missing a page	4	2	5	40
Operations	Old version	5	2	5	50
Engineering	Product level high	4	3	5	60
Compounding	Particle distribution low	3	4	5	60
Compounding	Particle distribution high	3	4	5	60
Engineering	Product level low	5	3	5	75

Change control[j]

Once the CGMP process has started, a change control program needs to be in place. But what is change control? This is a system that records and approves all changes regardless of how small or seemingly inconsequential they may be. This is one reason that current pharmaceutical practice is to perform commissioning activities prior to starting the formal GMP activities. Thus changes made during commissioning do not generally fall under the change control umbrella. As will be discussed in Chapter 7, commissioning tests are sometimes included in the installation qualification (IQ) and/or the operational qualification (OQ). If this is done with the approval for the quality unit (QU) and the commissioning document is officially signed, then these test results would be allowed (officially accepted) and there is no need

[j] S. Dara, "A Practical Guide to Change Control Systems Management", Journal of cGMP Compliance, Oct. 1999, V.4 #1 pp. 62–102; "Validation of Pharmaceutical Processes," 3rd Edition, Ed. By James P. Agalloco, Frederick J. Carleton, Chapter 9.

to retest these items as part of the IQ or OQ protocol. That is, commissioning documentation is not generally a CGMP function.

Change control affects all changes, not only a change made during an emergency but also a change made to improve the functioning of the unit. If you plan to utilize the "like for like" component of change control, then the two (or more) units need to be qualified and demonstrate that they can function as identically. Thus, if you are qualifying a pump and a tank as a stand-alone functioning unit and you want to be able to use two or more different pumps (just in case), then all of the pumps need to be qualified with the tank to demonstrate equal functionality. The IQ and OQ of each pump can be individual, but the performance qualification (PQ) needs to show similar results. So even if you have two pumps of equal output (not of the identical manufacturer), they cannot be used interchangeably on a given process system without a "joint" process qualification (except in emergency situations and under QU review). This leads to the need for "like for like" equipment. In that case, the process line is composed of identically functional units that can be "swapped out" as needed. However, a great deal of caution needs to be taken when claiming computer equipment is identical (see Chapter 5).

Investigations[k]

Another key quality system that needs to be in place prior to performing an equipment qualification is that of investigations. The investigation program needs to include investigations for the following:

* Any missed dates in a schedule
* Any deviation from the written procedure
* Any out of specification (OOS)—laboratory-derived or other
* Any deviation from the expected results of the testing

Generally speaking the ROOT CAUSE does not need to be reached for an investigation performed for a deviation uncovered in the IQ, OQ, or PQ, because it is very often very obvious. As an example a blue pump rather than a red pump is received. However, during manufacturing the ROOT CAUSE (or at least most probable cause) needs to be determined. This is one very important difference between a qualification investigation and a manufacturing investigation.

---

[k] B. Andersen & T. Fagerhaug, 'Root Cause Analysis—Simplified Tools and Techniques', 2nd Ed., American Society for Quality, 2006.

Deviations encountered during or part of the qualification program are often handled in a little different manner than deviations that occur during production. For example, deviations during production need to be logged and recorded as individual events and correlated to other similar events. A tracking program is used to track these events (not necessarily the one used for manufacturing investigations). In the case of deviations that occur during qualification testing, there is often just a log on the protocol in question, and the investigation is centered on resolving the deviation. This often results with interaction with the engineering department and/or operations to correct the problem. In either case a log of the event is needed, and a resolution to the protocol deviation needs to be completed before it can be signed off as approved for use.

Corrective action—Preventive action[1]

The CAPA program is important as it insures that the results of an investigation are correctly implemented. Thus, there are two phases to a CAPA program:

- In place
- In use

Corrective action is the immediate "fix" to the problem. For example, it may require revising an SOP. This is a long-term fix. The short-term fix in this case could be a "planned deviation" allowing the company to operate with the recommended change, for example, increased flow rate, prior to the SOP being revised and approved. If a planned deviation is used, it needs to be a short duration and very specific. Planned deviations are not a panacea for all problems. The preventive action is the "long-term fix" to the problem. Here again is maybe the revision of the SOP.

Once the preventive action is deemed to be "in place," it means that the corrective action (the immediate fix resulting from the investigation) has been implemented or at least started, whereas the term "in use" means that the preventive action (or the continuation of the corrective action) is being used correctly over time. This part is evaluated after a period of time such as 3 or 6 months.

---

[1] https://www.fda.gov/ICECI/Inspections/InspectionGuides/ucm170612.htm.

Calibration/metrology[m]

The "calibration program" is another quality system program that should be in place prior to starting the equipment qualification program. There are two calibrations that need to be considered. The first is the calibration of the instruments on the process equipment itself, and the second is the calibration of the test instruments to be used in the actual testing.

All instruments located on the process equipment itself need to be precalibrated prior to starting the OQ since some or all may be used in the actual test procedures. Calibration of process instrumentation is usually performed during the commissioning of the unit so that you know that the unit is performing correctly when placed in operation. For example, it is not necessary to install a pressure gauge in a line if one exists on the equipment already and it is calibrated.

Test instruments need to be calibrated prior to the test performed and again after the test. This is to demonstrate that the test instrument has remained in calibration during the testing. For example, a tachometer used to measure the speed of an agitator should be calibrated prior to the test and after the test. This applies to test instruments like thermocouples, while the unit the thermocouples are attached to (the recorder) can usually be calibrated only once a year depending on the manufacturer specifications.

Calibration of critical instruments (those absolutely needed for the process to function correctly) is often completed at least every 6 months, whereas all other instruments can be calibrated as needed (as determined by regular testing).

Scheduled calibrations according to a written program and performed according to a written SOP cannot be missed and still have the unit considered operational. If a scheduled calibration is missed, an investigation needs to be performed to determine the reason for the missed calibration. The unit cannot be used until calibrated according to the SOP, and the investigation is closed.

Preventive maintenance[n]

While the preventative maintenance program need not be in use for commissioning on the particular unit being qualified, it certainly needs to be

---

[m] https://www.pharmamanufacturing.com/assets/wp_downloads/pdf/Vaisala_quality.pdf.

[n] Hao Yinghua, Liang Yi, "Targeted Preventive Maintenance of Pharmaceutical Equipment" Journal of Drug Design and Medicinal Chemistry, 2018; 4(2): 10–15 http://www.sciencepublishinggroup.com/j/jddmc.

in place upon completion of the qualification. This is assuming that the unit is new and is not being repurposed.

The preventive maintenance program is first based on the manufacturer recommendations for the specific unit. Each unit should have a defined maintenance schedule, just as your car does. Some items such as lubrication may be required weekly, annually, or something in between. The vendor will or should supply the frequency for this. After the unit has been in use for a period of time, adjustments may be made to the preventive maintenance schedule. In no case should a scheduled maintenance be skipped. This would lead to a deficiency and thus an investigation.

Cleaning[o]

Keeping the equipment clean is an important part of the qualification process. While cleaning is not needed for the IQ portion of the program, it may be needed for the OQ and certainly the PQ portions of the program. The reason for keeping the equipment clean is another way to assure that the correct test results are achieved. There may be tests that require the use of the product that may influence further testing.

While cleaning verification and certainly cleaning validation are not required at the IQ, clean equipment is a critical aspect of completing the qualification program. Depending on the testing to be performed during the OQ, a cleaning verification may be necessary. This entails swabbing or rinsing the unit to remove any nonproduct material that may impact the testing. However, when performing the PQ tests (when necessary), cleaning verification, to show that the equipment is cleanable, is important to do. This is because cleaning validation becomes a big part of the process validation program.[p]

Document control

A robust document control system is another quality system that should be in place prior to starting a qualification program. It is critical to know the status of all documents being prepared and the status of all documents being executed.

---

[o] Guide to Inspections of Cleaning Validation, FDA, July 1993.
[p] S. Ostrove—"How to Validate a Pharmaceutical Process", Academic Press, 2016.

The person(s) tasked with the execution of the protocol should be sure to obtain a complete set of the protocols or those sections assigned, prior to starting the execution. All pages need to be accounted for, and copies of the original should be used for all executions. The document control group/department needs to maintain a careful and complete record of all documents in and out and all copies (e.g., sign out/in unless it is fully electronic and under 21 CFR Part 11). Remember whenever copies are used, they need to be marked as "copy" before use in the field.

Re-qualification

As stated in Chapter 1, requalification is not needed except in certain situations (includes but not limited to):
- There is a significant change to the equipment.
    o A change is needed that takes the unit outside of the proven acceptable range (PAR).
- The equipment has been moved (even a little).
    o NOTE: A full qualification is usually not required; however, a check on calibrations, utility connections, and components are just some of the checks necessary.
- Temperature mapping needs to be confirmed (e.g., autoclaves and tunnels).
    o Checking to determine if the hot and cold areas already mapped during the qualification remain the same.
- There is a change is the process (requiring the equipment to be run at a previously nonqualified condition)

CHAPTER FOUR

Equipment design considerations

In order to have an easy qualification, the equipment needs to be designed properly. The first step in designing process equipment is to consult with the users (operations). They need to tell the process engineers the specific use of the equipment. For example, a tank is needed to hold 500 gal of liquid with a pH below 5.0. The user is expected to be able to give specifics as to volume, flow rate needed, etc. They know what the process is and will be based on the development reports from the R&D group. (NOTE: Keep in mind that according to the 2011 FDA Process Validation Guideline,[a] all development, including equipment design, is now included in the full process validation program.[b]) For examples of user specifications, see Table 1.

Not only is equipment design important for the proper operation of the process itself, but it also directly impacts its qualification. The qualification group should be included as part of the design process so as to assure that all aspects of the unit will be tested appropriately and that requalification, if necessary, can be achieved with minimal effort. For example, if an autoclave is to be ordered or a tank to be built, the qualification team should have input as to some specific requirements, for example, a validation port on the autoclave or the welds used for sample ports on the tank. In the design process, not only the actual function of the equipment but also its cleaning, its maintenance, and its calibration need to be considered. These factors are also part of the unit's complete qualification.

In the design of a piece of process equipment, not only the reaction chemistry but also the physical and thermodynamic properties of the reaction have to be considered. Is the unit to be under pressure or vacuum? If so, does it have the required ASTM rating? Some other considerations overlap into cleaning validation, computer system validation, and process validation.

Regardless of the similarities in the equipment (i.e., tanks are tanks), each type of equipment has its own unique design requirements. As can be

[a]Guidance for Industry—Process Validation: General Principles and Practice, FDA, Jan. 2011.
[b]S. Ostrove, "How to Validate a Pharmaceutical Process", Academic Press, 2016.

Equipment Qualification in the Pharmaceutical Industry
https://doi.org/10.1016/B978-0-12-817568-2.00004-X

Table 1 Examples of user specifications

Physical
- Speed
- Temperature
- Mix times
- Volumes to be used
- Flow rates (e.g., chromatography systems)

Chemical
- Chemicals to be used
- Cleaning agents
- Length of contact time

Thermodynamic
- Gassing rate (bioreactors)
- Heating rates needed—time
- Cooling rate needed—time

---

ascertained in 21CRF 211.63,[c] the equipment "…shall be of appropriate design, adequate size, and suitably located…" "for its intended use." This is taken to mean that the equipment needs to be designed for its specific purpose. This does not preclude using a piece of equipment for multiple processes or using a stock unit made for multiple purposes. However, the amount of material in the reaction and the ability to maintain temperature and flows need to be established and shown to be appropriate for its intended use. 21 CFR 211.65(a)[d] takes this further by stating that the materials of construction "…shall not be reactive, additive, or absorptive…." This means that the materials of construction (MOC) should not in any way change or alter the process reaction or the product.

Table 2 lists some basic questions that should be included as part of the process/equipment design. These questions can come from either the users or the process engineers. Other questions may arise during design that may be answered by either the user's needs or the R&D group. For examples, see Table 2.

After consulting with the users of the equipment, the process engineers need to consider needed design characteristics. The first rule of thumb is that if you don't want to overdesign (or underdesign), don't use equipment that is too large or too small for your process. Make sure that the operation group is also included in the design phase of the equipment so that all user

---

[c]Code of Federal Regulations (CFR) Subpart D specifically 21 Part 211 §63.
[d]Code of Federal Regulations (CFR) Subpart D 21 Part 211 §65.

Table 2 Some basic design question

- What are the user's requirements?
- Can the unit serve its expected purpose?
- Can it be cleaned effectively/safely?
  o Can it be disassembled/assembled easily?
- Are there special instruments needed to test its function?
- Can it be placed in an area that is environmentally correct for its operation?
- Are there special requirements for mounting or positioning the unit?
- Do the users or validation specialists know the key or major components for its operation?
- Size/location
  o Capacity/volume
  o Support structures (concrete, wall mounts, etc.)
  o Space requirements
- Temperature/flow maintenance
- Controls
  o Manual
  o Microchip
  o Programmed logic controller (PLC)
  o Supervisory control and data acquisition (SCADA)
- Cleaning
  o Clean hold time
  o Dirty hold time
  o Ease of disassembly
  o Clean in place (CIP) versus clean out of place (COP)
- Environmental
  o Storage—clean
  o Storage—dirty
  o Where used
- Maintenance
  o Preventive maintenance program
  o Emergency
- Portable versus nonportable
- Attachments to other units in the process (e.g., welds and flanges)

requirements (URS) can be met. For example, a tank that needs to hold 100 gal of reaction mixture should be sized to hold 150–175 gal (+50%–75%) of liquid. Make sure that the impeller (agitator) will reach a point near the bottom of the tank for proper agitation and that the fill and exit ports are large enough to fill and empty the unit efficiently (Table 3). Other things that may need to be considered are the following:

- Design the speed controls so that the range to be used is included in the liner portion of the control curve.

Table 3 Process engineer design considerations

- Size/location
  - o Capacity/volume
  - o Support structures (concrete, wall mounts, etc.)
  - o Space requirements
- Temperature/flow maintenance
- Controls
  - o Manual
  - o Microchip
  - o Programmed logic controller (PLC)
  - o Supervisory control and data acquisition (SCADA)
- Cleaning
  - o Clean hold time
  - o Dirty hold time
  - o Ease of disassembly
  - o Clean in place (CIP) versus clean out of place (COP)
- Environmental
  - o Storage—clean
  - o Storage—dirty
  - o Where used
- Maintenance
  - o Preventive maintenance program
  - o Emergency
- Portable versus nonportable
- Attachments to other units in the process (e.g., welds and flanges)

- Are the heating units
  - o too large or small?
  - o able to be controlled to the correct temperature to make an effective seal on the blister?
- Are they correctly placed?
- Are the caps torqued to the correct degree?
- Can all areas of the tank be reached for proper cleaning (baffles, tops, ports, etc.)?
- Avoid dead legs (Fig. 1).[e]

After completing the design requirements of the equipment, the unit specifications are usually sent to a vendor for a bid on its construction (note: depending on the equipment, construction may be in-house). These bids should be reviewed for CGMP and other regulatory needs before they are submitted to the vendor by the qualification/validation group. Depending on the process, the cleaning, or the thermodynamics to be

[e]A dead leg is per WHO.org http://apps.who.int/medicinedocs/en/d/Js14060e/16.html.

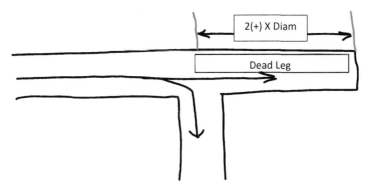

Fig. 1 Example of a dead leg.

encountered by the unit, the vendor will need to be appraised of this prior to bidding on the unit so that the proper material of construction can be used. When the bids from the vendors are received back, they should be again reviewed not only for price but also for conformance with user specifications requested and CGMP compliance. Where this bid review is not done, or is incomplete, problems may be found during commissioning or even during the qualification process, which can greatly slow or even stop a construction program and delay product reaching the market. After an appropriate bid review, the selected vendor will fabricate the unit.

Materials of construction

As discussed earlier the specific use of the unit is a must consideration when designing a piece of process equipment. The material of construction as noted in 21CFR211.65[f] is critical to all operations. In most cases the industry choice of material is stainless steel (SS). Keep in mind the various qualities of SS. For example, there are 304, 316, and 316L; the class depends on the amount of chromium, nickel, carbon, and other metals in the stainless-steel formulation. Depending on the product and the position of the unit in the process, any may be acceptable. However, for most pharmaceutical operations, 316L is the one most often used for piping, tanks, and other process equipment. Other popular choices for production equipment are glass-lined vessels, polytetrafluoroethylene (PTFE),[g] or Hastelloy[h] (resistant to most organics, acids, bases, etc.).

[f]ibid.
[g]http://www.crp.co.uk/technical.aspx.
[h]https://www.titanmf.com/alloys/applications-of-hastelloy/.

Cleaning agents to be used in the cleaning process may also affect the composition of the unit construction. As noted in the succeeding text, halides will erode stainless steel, and some acids will dissolve glass (HF).

Other product contact materials that need to be considered are the materials used in the primary packaging and consequent product safety. For example, blister packages need heat to seal the blister to the base. How thick is the blister material? Will it let too much air into the package or too little? Will the heat damage the product?

Location[i]

Location from both an environmental perspective and equipment repair or maintenance perspective is part of the equipment qualification process and is included as part of the installation qualification (IQ) protocol. Items such as air flow for cooling, ability to open ports or lids, or even the ability to disassemble and assemble the unit for cleaning are just some examples that need to be considered in designing the equipment. Is the location environmentally sound for the operation over a long period of time (temperature and humidity)?

Another consideration is cleaning or replacing piping connected to a larger piece of equipment. Fig. 2 shows sanitary links that connect piping to tanks and other units in the process.

Consideration also needs to be given to the manner of mounting the unit. Wall mounts will require shims to allow proper operation; floor mounts may require specific thickness of concrete pads or vibration-absorbing materials. Are the unit's legs to be bolted down, or are they to be pointed so as to present as little contact area for cleaning, as in a clean room?

Cleaning and maintenance[j]

While equipment qualification does not actually include cleaning verification or validation, it is certainly an important consideration when planning and designing a piece of process equipment. The unit must be cleaned between uses and verified to have removed to an acceptable level both the API and the excipients. Connections to large units (tanks, e.g., before tanks) need to have piping that is short enough to be easily cleaned (Fig. 2) but not

[i]Code of Federal Regulations (CFR) Subpart D, 21 Part 211 §63.
[j]Code of Federal Regulations (CFR) Subpart D, 21 Part 211 §67.

Fig. 2 Sanitary fitting connecting a tank.

too short to add possibilities of contamination upon disassembly. Note in this figure that the length of piping is short allowing for complete cleaning not only of the pipe but also of the valve attached to the tank.

A major consideration when selecting the material to be used is the cleaning or removal of all components (active pharmaceutical ingredients and excipients). SS is susceptible to degradation (pitting) from halides[k] (F, Br, Cl, I, and At) when they are combined with other metals (NA, K, etc.). Other materials, as mentioned earlier, can be used such as glass, PTFE, or Hastelloy depending on temperatures or chemicals to be used in that process step, the cleaning agents (halides, detergents, solvents, etc.).

Cleaning of tanks or other large items may require cleaning-in-place (CIP) procedures or sanitize-in-place (SIP) systems. Testing to assure that all areas are completely covered and clean is often done through the use of riboflavin at 100 ppm.[l] It is also necessary to assure that all welds or other

[k]Pitting corrosion of martensitic stainless steel in halide bearing solutions, S.Pahlavan, S.MoazenI, TajiK. Saffar, M.Hamrah, M.H.Moayed, S.Mollazadeh Beidokhti; Corrosion Science, Vol. 112, Nov. 2016, pp. 233–240.
[l]www.abprocess.com.

connections of piping, etc. are smooth internally and externally so as to min-imize surface area for chemical or bioburden buildup. This applies to the all product contact surfaces regardless of material of construction. This is why passivation is usually required.

Maintenance of the equipment is also a critical aspect to the design pro-cess. As discussed earlier, in location, the ability to get to all sides or areas of the unit for maintenance is just as important as the actual design. This is also the precursor for the preventive maintenance (PM) program that is one of the quality systems that will be part of an FDA audit.

Other considerations

There are some other considerations when designing or specifying a piece of process equipment, for example, location of the instruments asso-ciated with the unit, calibration based on criticality of these instruments, and the preventive maintenance program needed to maintain the unit in full GMP compliance.

Where product is or may be exposed to the environment, the units need to be covered for their operation so that the product is protected (i.e., objects falling into tanks or onto process lines (Fig. 3) or into bottles during filling

Fig. 3 Covered operation.

from above). In other cases, the product needs to be protected from the operators, or the operators need to be protected from the product. The design of these protective coverings will vary from very simple as in Fig. 3 to more elaborate using plexiglass or other materials based on the product (cosmetic, OTC, or parenteral) on the use but need to be included in the design of the equipment since workers may still need access to the unit for adjustments, cleaning, or maintenance (Fig. 3).

Still, other items that need consideration in process equipment design are the following:

- Internal wall smoothness (cleaning, flow, etc.)
- Possibility of dead legs[e]
- Turbulent versus linear flow of materials
- Weld type (smoothness and material used for the weld)
- Drainability
- Flexibility
- Portability

Obviously, the list can contain numerous items depending on the product, the materials used in its production, cleaning requirements of the product and excipients, etc. Again, as always, think about the design as a vital aspect of production not just a vessel or unit to perform a function such as holding a liquid.

CHAPTER FIVE

Equipment controls and automation

Computer or automated control systems for pharmaceutical process equipment are almost ubiquitous in the industry.[a] It seems that every piece of equipment has or is associated with some sort of automated or computer control. This chapter is presented to give the reader a basic understanding of what and how and where to include (or certainly consider) computer system validation (CSV) as part of the equipment qualification program. It is not intended to be a full CSV guide. While computer systems are often referred to as a validation program for the most part, it really is a qualification—since computers or computer systems can be treated as equipment not processes. There are many good references for CSV (e.g., GAMP5[b] or the PDA TR18[c]). This chapter will provide information as to what to include or at least be aware of the need when qualifying your process equipment.

In considering the qualification level (Per GAMP-5) or the extent of structural versus functional (see later) qualification, there is always a question as to whether, how, or where to qualify a computer-controlled unit or automated system—should it be qualified as a separate independent unit or as a functional piece of the equipment? Should the equipment be qualified as a separate unit or its qualification be included into the process equipment itself? The answer here is not always easy and will take some thought and understanding of the computer or controllers' actual function. In any case, the controller or computer system must be qualified. One aspect of the analysis on the approach to take is to ask, "How integrated into the operation of the unit is the control system, and can it be removed from the unit and have the equipment have some functional value?" Thus—for example, the programmed logic controller (PLC) that controls an autoclave—while relatively easily removed from the autoclave, the autoclave will not function at

---

[a]"Validation of Pharmaceutical Processes," 3rd Ed, edited by James P. Agalloco, Frederick J. Carleton. Chapter 47.
[b]GAMP 5 A Risk-Based Approach to Compliant GxP Computerized Systems ISPE, 2008.
[c]Parenteral Drug Association, Technical Report 18, "Validation of Computer-Related Systems", Vol. 49, 1995.

35

all without the PLC, and the PLC will not function for its, or other purposes, since it is programmed for the specific autoclave. Thus, the autoclave PLC is usually qualified as a major component of the autoclave. On the other hand, a PLC that functions for a laboratory information management system (LIMS) is used to collect data from a variety of laboratory units. This system is mostly qualified or validated alone since each unit connected to the LIMS can function independently and data can be obtained with or without the LIMS. The distinction is the function of the computer system control.

As stated, there is some sort of computer control for almost every piece of process equipment. Controls range from microchips all the way through full computer controls (e.g., supervisory control and data acquisition— SCADA). It is important to include some type of qualification of any type of "computer or automation" control into the IQ and OQ protocols. For those controlled by a microchip (e.g., vibrating shaker) or erasable programmable read-only memory (EPROM—not changeable or programmable by the user), functional testing only is usually an acceptable approach. A slightly more advanced controller is the electronically erasable programmable read-only memory (EEPROM—which is reprogrammable with another computer program) that could have its functionality tested as part of the unit operation. An example of this type of unit is a programmable fraction collector. Keep in mind that structural testing is not always possible.

So, what is structural testing or qualification as compared with functional testing or qualification? Both need to be completed, at least to some degree, prior to considering the qualification complete.

Structural qualification

A definition found in the Pharmaceutical Inspection Co-operation Scheme (PIC/S) is as follows:

> *Examining the internal structure of the source code. Includes low-level and high-level code review, path analysis, auditing of programming procedures and standards actually used, inspection for extraneous "dead code", boundary analysis and other techniques. Requires specific computer science and programming expertise.*[d]

This refers to the software itself. A full structural qualification includes, but not limited to, the following:

[d]Good Practices for Computerized Systems in Regulated "GXP" Environments, PIC/S 011-3, 25 September 2007.

- Source code (for computer programs) review
- Ladder logic (for programmed logic controllers) review
- Programming language
- Structure of the written code
- Annotations in the code
- Review for dead code
- Software version installed
- Number of users

From the preceding text, it is clear that a full structural qualification may be difficult to achieve on most software. Only software programs that are either written in-house or by a third party contracted to write the code (BESPEC) can have a complete structural review. Software purchased from a third party that is configurable (configurable off the shelf—COTS) usually has a modified structural review. This leads to what is called "gray-box qualification" (more on this later).

Functional qualification

As the term indicates, this involves the actual physical testing of the computer system. Some very simple operating systems, a microchip operating a vibrating shaker (as in the preceding text), cannot have a separate functional test. Testing here would be through the unit itself. On the other hand, more complex computer system (e.g., running a blender or controlling the temperature and agitation of a tank) can be functionally tested as a separate unit and then combined with the process unit. The fact that the computer or PLC communicates with the agitator or the heat exchanger (heating unit) has different functions than demonstrating that the tank is able to maintain temperature or that the agitator maintains correct missing speed.

Both a full structural and a full functional test of the computer system or control constitute what is referred to as a "white box" qualification. This is actually not very common today since most software is written by a third party who limits access to the source code or ladder logic.[e] There are two other types of qualification often referred to for computer system qualification. These are "gray box" and "black box." These are the most common types of qualification today.

The gray-box qualification is a full functional testing and a partial structural testing of the software. In this case the structural testing may constitute

[e]Ladder logic is the equivalent of the source code for a Programmed Logic Controller (PLC).

verifying that the correct software was installed by verifying the software name and version number. In comparison, the black-box qualification is often applied to COTS systems or primarily functional testing of the software only. That is, does the software function as expected, and does it meet the expected user requirements?

Black box, gray box, white box qualifications

From the earlier discussion, it should be clear that there are three types of full computer system qualification/validation (for systems that are accessible for source code or ladder logic review), that is, computers or PLCs that are accessible. For those systems that contain computers or PLCs that are not easily accessible (e.g., autoclaves), BLACK-BOX testing is usually acceptable. For this, one needs only to verify the version of software installed and to perform functional testing to demonstrate that the program performs as expected.

Going up a notch to GRAY-BOX testing, one needs to not only verify the version of the program installed but also confirm as much code information as possible. This can usually be performed with source code or ladder logic written specifically for the operation or equipment (e.g., COTS systems).

When WHITE-BOX testing is able to be performed, a full evaluation of the source code or ladder logic needs to be conducted. This, as described earlier, requires full access to the source code or ladder logic so that dead code, annotations, etc. can be evaluated.

IQ/OQ for computer or automated systems

Because of some of the complexity of a computer or automated control system, a procedure has been developed to help assure compliant qualification and is referred to as the traceability matrix (TM) (Table 1).

Table 1 Basic trace matrix contents

- CPP or function
- URS location
- FRS
- DDS location
- IQ section
- OQ section
- PQ section

This, as seen in Fig. 1, lists the user requirements (URS), the functional requirements (FS or FRS), and the design requirements (DR or DDS) as well as the location of the testing to be performed in the IQ and OQ and or PQ. Fig. 1 gives an example of a TM chart that can be used for computer/automated systems or process equipment. By completing the TM, it is easier to assure that all functions and operations will be correctly tested in the appropriate protocol.

Example of a trace matrix

Function/CPP	URS	FRS	DS	IQ	OQ	PQ
Security	1.0	3.2	7.4	4	3	–
Adds col 1 and 2	3	5.7	10.3	5	6	2
Full mixed[a]	7	9	11.8	–	7	9

Note: The numbers are arbitrary and do not apply to any real document.
[a]This is a CPP not a computer function.

Fig. 1 Example of a simple TM.

Table 2 IQ considerations[a]

- Size
- Location
- Physical equipment
    - All components (hard drives, cards, ports, etc.)
- Security present
- Environment
- Network connection
- Power requirements
    - Emergency
- Structural testing
- Software
    - Version
    - Source code review
    - Users
- Vendor
    - Audit—experience
    - Language used
- Number of users
- Input type (alpha or numeric or both)

[a]Includes but not limited to.

Table 3 Generalized OQ considerations[a]

- Hardware
  - Power limits
  - Power failure recovery
  - Environmental stress
  - Alarms
  - All component functions
- Software
  - Input limits (boundaries)
- Functional testing
- Security test
  - Log in/out
- Operation of input and output devices (keyboard, screen, ports, etc.)
- Data recovery (local—e.g., hard drive)
  - Data recovery after storage
- Alarms, locks
- Part 11 (audit trail)

---

[a]Includes but not limited to.

Wherever possible the computer control needs to have an IQ and OQ prepared. Table 2 gives a list of items to be included in the IQ, and Table 3 gives a list of items to be included in the OQ.

It is important to note that there are other tests that need to be performed on computer systems that do not exist on other pieces of equipment (e.g., tanks). Table 4 shows a list of these tests. Two tests are more unique to computer systems qualification than any other piece of equipment. These tests are the electromagnetic and radio frequency interference (EMI and RFI)

Table 4 Other possible testing

- Electromagnetic interference (EMI)
- Radio frequency interference (RFI)
- I/O loops
- Security—biometric or standard
  - Data lines
  - Networks
  - Users
- Data integrity
  - Data in versus data out
- Robustness
- Reproducibility

---

tests. These tests can be and are usually performed with common equipment found in the plant. These two tests, using common equipment, for example, an electric drill (for EMI testing) and the handheld radios used by employees (for RFI testing), can easily demonstrate that the computer or controller is free from this kind of interference. These tests are important in order to demonstrate complete data integrity during working time.

Part 11

Still another very important aspect of computer qualification is the question of Part 11[f] integrity. Does the software act in a way to store or transmit data? An example here is an HPLC system that is computer controlled. The unit may produce a paper tape of the chromatogram that is inserted into the laboratory notebook. In addition, the unit may store the chromatogram in the LIMS system for further analysis (e.g., integration of the peaks). In the former case, if the paper tape is the final record of the test performed, then Part 11 is not a requirement; however, if it is the latter case, then Part 11 is definitely a requirement in the qualification process.

As stated in CFR Part 11 (21 CFR 11.1(b)), this applies to "…records in electronic form that are created, modified, maintained, archived, retrieved, or transmitted…." In other words, this applies to anything that has to do with electronic records or signatures. Electronic signatures pertain to signatures that are included by electronic means. Further guidance on Part 11 requirements can be found in the FDA guidelines on Part 11.[g]

Summary

From the earlier discussion, it should be clear that the qualification of computer or automated controls for a piece of process equipment is necessary and is not very different than any other qualification. Today, due to the complexity of the controls and programming, many systems are qualified by either the Gray- or Black-box approach. If the software is prepared in-house, then White-box qualification certainly should be completed.

[f]FDA 21 CFR Part 11—Electronic Records; Electronic Signatures.
[g]Guidance for Industry Part 11, Electronic Records; Electronic Signatures—Scope and Application, August 2003.

Computer systems are nothing to be afraid of. Common sense and an understanding of what it does (as in with all pharmaceutical equipment) will enable the necessary testing to complete the qualification. The physical unit (keyboard, screen, ports, etc.) make up the IQ, while testing these to be sure that the data are correct and that the computer does what it is supposed to do (i.e., open/close a valve, start/stop an operation at a specific time, etc.) is the OQ.

CHAPTER SIX

Preparing the protocols: General approach

According to Merriam-Webster online dictionary, a protocol is "a detailed plan of a scientific or medical experiment, treatment, or procedure."[a] This means that prior to performing any commissioning or qualification work on any piece of equipment, a formal protocol needs to be prepared.[b] Also, this definition clearly fits with the FDA's prospective validation/qualification approach; the tests are predefined, as are the expected results. All protocols are designed around the needs to the use or process as defined by the users (operations/production), that is, the user specifications. According to the FDA, all protocols need to be prepared on using good science and a risk basis approach.[c]

Protocol development

Before we look at specific protocols, let's look at the general path needed to get a protocol approved for execution. Fig. 1 outlines such a flow.

This flow diagram is a generalized approach. The flowchart shows the generally expected time and responsibilities for developing a protocol. (Note: not every protocol needs to follow this path as outlined nor the time line indicated. This may depend on whether the protocol is prepared in-house or by an outside firm.)

However, there are some general approaches that have proved successful over the years.[d] The first step is that the person assigned to prepare the protocol should be familiar with the intended function of the unit and then to inquire from the users (if possible) as to the units expected specific function.

---

[a]https://www.merriam-webster.com/dictionary/protocol.
[b]21 CFR 211.100.
[c]FDA, Pharmaceutical CGMPs for the 21st Century—A Risk Based Approach, Sept. 2004.
[d]https://www.pharmaceuticalonline.com/doc/writing-compliant-iq-oq-pq-protocols-meeting-fda-expectations-0001.

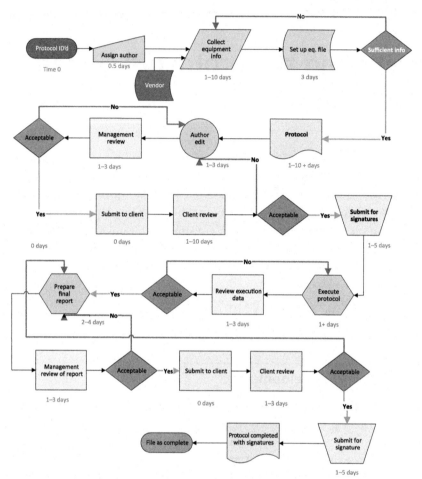

Fig. 1 General flow of a protocol development.

There are several other questions and things to do in order to make the preparation easier and more effective:

- Review the PFD to understand the general process flow.
- Review the P&ID to confirm the system boundaries (Figs. 2 and 3).
- Review the FAT, SAT, and commissioning tests that were performed and the process development/history (e.g., closely related products being manufactured on expected similar equipment).
- Determine if any other machines are in use of a similar type.
- Ask if there are any other protocols or products similar to the one to be manufactured in that unit currently in use that uses similar equipment.

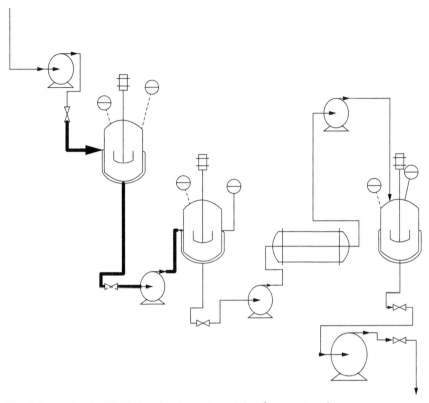

Fig. 2 Example of a P&ID showing incoming piping for a protocol.

And finally, they should rereview current FDA guidelines[e] and current warning letters[f] to be sure that all necessary aspects are covered. By understanding the FDA's expectations as outlined in Table 1, a clear, concise protocol can be prepared.

Once the earlier questions and checks are completed, the author can begin protocol preparation. Protocols need to have a specific defined structure or format. This format is not as important as content. However, once a format has been established for the company, do try to maintain this format for future protocols.

A general table of contents can be seen in Table 2. Certainly, each protocol will have its own unique table of contents where each item or test would be listed.

[e]Process Validation Guide, others.
[f]https://www.fda.gov/ICECI/EnforcementActions/WarningLetters/default.htm.

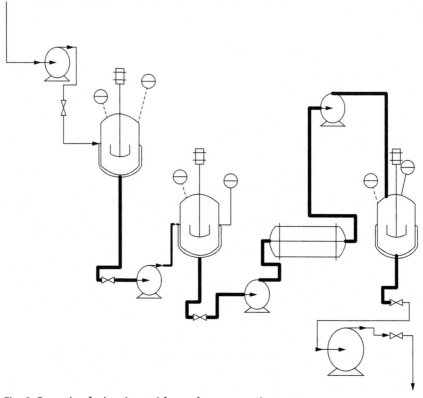

Fig. 3 Example of a header and footer for a protocol page.

Table 1 General FDA expectations

- Written SOPs are available
  - IQ needs a list
  - OQ needs a draft
  - PQ needs them signed
- Prepare protocols (review and approve) in ADVANCE
  - Risk-based
  - Use GOOD science
- Criteria MUST be measurable
- Obtain *approved* protocol **BEFORE** executing
- Have the final validation report—APPROVED
- VALID CONCLUSION FROM THE ACTUAL RESULTS

Table 2 Sample: Table of contents

- Title/approval
- Purpose
- Scope
- Specific tests
  - IQ—All physical parameters
    - All persons executing the protocol need to sign or initial their respective action at the time they perform the task as at the performed by at the bottom of each section
  - OQ—All operating needs—full range of operation
    - Each test is usually a separate page or section and requires a performed by and reviewed by signature
  - PQ—Time testing/stability per specific production use
- Results
- References

Layout

Each protocol (IQ, OQ, or PQ) has its own layout or configuration. This is not critical to the actual acceptance of the protocol or unit for its operation or function in the process. But once a layout has been established, as stated, it should be maintained as much as possible. Each protocol should have a header and footer. The header should at least indicate the protocol name and document number (unique so it is traceable), the identity of the protocol, the version number, and usually the company name. The footer should have at least the page number in the format of Page X of Y[g] and any other information desired such as file route and date of preparation (Fig. 4). Remember that all pages need to have a unique number and that when copies are used for execution, they be clearly marked as copies. The PQ protocol is designed as the IQ or OQ, but more specific tests for the unit operation for the product are listed not just the operation of the unit. Another general consideration for protocol preparation is that only one side of a page is used. This avoids errors when making copies.

[g]21 CFR 211.105 and FDA Guidance for Industry M4: Organization of the CTD.

Header

Company name or logo	Equip. name 'IXXXXXXXX' Qualification protocol	Page 1 of 2	
Protocol No.:	Effective Date:	Revision No.: A	Supersedes: None

Footer

Valid for 24 h from: date/time	Page 1 of 6	4/13/19

Fig. 4 Header and footer example.

Stand-alone conditions

Another important aspect of protocol preparation is to make sure that the protocol is designed around what is known as a "stand-alone system." Examples of stand-alone systems would be a refrigerator or autoclave. A stand-alone system means that all valves, piping, instruments, equipment (tanks, pumps, etc.), etc. that make up the system are included in a protocol. There are two basic ways to achieve stand-alone conditions:

1. All piping, instruments, etc. entering the unit (following a valve that can isolate the unit) are to be included with the unit's protocol (Fig. 2).
2. The other way is to include all piping, instruments, etc. leaving the unit as part (up to a valve that can isolate the unit) of the unit's protocol (Fig. 3).

No other component is needed for its function (other than possibly a utility such as electricity). Developing "system boundaries" is the means to achieving this stand-alone state. Using the P&IDs, one can draw with colored markers (or others) lines to demark the components to be included or excluded from a given protocol. This will assure that **all** components (piping, valves, pumps, etc.) are accounted for in a protocol (it doesn't matter which protocol). Keeping this in mind, each protocol set (IQ/OQ/PQ) should be specific for the unit being qualified.

A totally generic approach to preparing a protocol (e.g., all tests or sections are identical for all equipment) is not usually acceptable. Thus, having the same sections and/or tests for all IQs or OQs may not actually test or verify the unit as carefully as it needs to be tested. This said, each protocol needs to be as specific and unique to the unit tested as possible.

Table 3 Acceptance criteria

- Measurable
- Quantitative
- Comparisons of clinical materials (i.e., bio-batch, impurity profile, and R&D)
- Capable of controlling process parameters within acceptable ranges
- Variability assessed using SPC methods during development

Acceptance criteria[h]

Acceptance criteria for all protocols need to be quantitative and measurable (as expressed in Table 3). For example, when turning on a unit and the indicator light changes from RED to GREEN is a measurable, quantitative result. Another important aspect of acceptance criterion is that they should be expressed as a range. For example, the temperature of the solution reaches $45°C \pm 2°C$. As compared with saying that the temperature goes up or down, one needs to know how much. It can say it goes up at least $X°C$ or not more than $X°C$ or even not less than $X°C$ nor more than $X°C$. However, the set point can and should be a definite value, for example, $45°C$, which is the target for that particular operation.

Protocol review

All protocols will need to be reviewed and approved not only by the author but also by others. This leads to the signature requirements on the protocol. There are two signature pages found on all protocols. The first signature page is the preapproval page that indicates that the items (tests or specifications and acceptance criteria) in the protocol are acceptable to those signing. The signature page at the end of the protocol is by the same persons or groups that signed the preapproval page and indicates that the results are acceptable and true.

So, who needs to sign a protocol? The author certainly needs to assume credit for the protocol, so they sign as the preparer. Then, depending on the protocol type and the unit function, usually, someone (a manager or supervisor level person) from operations, engineering, and possibly maintenance will also review and approve. These reviewers review the document for their expertise only. That is, the engineering person will attest that the unit

[h]21 CFR 210.3(20).

can operate at the conditions specified (e.g., speed, temperature, pressure, or vacuum.). The operation person will attest that the test criteria and acceptance criteria include those needed for production. If there are safety items (e.g., interlocks), then the safety group should also sign and affirm that the unit can meet the requirements of safety required. The last person or group to sign both the preapproval and postapproval page is always the quality unit. They review the protocol for compliance to corporate standards of writing, FDA requirements for protocols, and other in-house or specific requirements for the protocol. Their review is based on meeting both corporate and regulatory requirements. This is done for both the preapproval page of the document (it certifies that the protocol meets the requirements of all parties concerned with the correct operation of the unit(s)) and the postapproval page (the same departments review the data to assure that they are accurate and meet the acceptance criteria set forth).

Each test section needs to have a space for the person(s) executing the protocol and the person reviewing each section and a comment area. This review is not to be confused with the approval pages. It is to indicate primarily that all spaces on the document were filled in, that the data appear correct, and that the acceptance criteria were either met as understood by the reviewer. This review should be performed as soon as possible after the execution so as to be able to correct any errors or answer any questions (refer to Chapter 10).

CHAPTER SEVEN

Commissioning and decommissioning

With the basic understanding of preparing a protocol (Chapter 6), it is now necessary to consider some of the specific protocols needed for a full qualification program. These include the Factory Acceptance Test[a] (FAT), the Site Acceptance Test (SAT), and the Commissioning Protocols. Table 1 summarizes the key events of the equipment life cycle for all types of equipment starting with establishing the need and ending with the unit being taken off line and sold or discarded (even if it is a used piece of equipment).

FAT and SAT

From this table, it can be seen that there is a lot to activity prior to testing the unit. This all needs to be documented. The FAT and SAT testing are the forerunners to commissioning. After the unit is ordered and the (qualified/approved) vendor is ready to ship to the client, the FAT protocol is usually run. The FAT protocol is usually prepared by the vendor; however, the client company can also prepare the protocol. The FAT is prepared mostly for large items such as an autoclave. Even so, smaller units (e.g., glass washer or a V-blender) may be initially tested on the vendor site before it is shipped to the client. The company, prior to the start of any FAT testing, should review the FAT and approve the protocol and add their own specific requirements if necessary. This is because the vendor will probably prepare the FAT protocol so that the unit will pass. Thus the company should have prearranged agreement with the vendor to be able to add, or change, any of the tests so as to best evaluate the unit's operation as required by their specific process. It is also advisable for a representative of the contracting company (company) to attend the testing to witness the testing and to be sure that any changes to the FAT that were required by the company are included and that the testing meets manufacturing needs. Once the FAT is completed and approved, the unit is shipped to the company.

[a] http://carelabz.com/what-factory-acceptance-testing-how-fat-done/.

Equipment Qualification in the Pharmaceutical Industry
https://doi.org/10.1016/B978-0-12-817568-2.00007-5

Table 1 General equipment life cycle

- Need established
- Process engineers determine design specifications
- Design specifications are reviewed by operations and sent to purchasing
- Order equipment from a qualified vendor
- Vendor submits drawings/specifications with bid
- Bid is reviewed for company requirements
- Order is placed
- Perform Factory Acceptance Test (FAT)
- Perform Site Acceptance Test (SAT)
- Commission the unit
- Qualify the unit (Chapter 8)
- Use the unit
- Decommission when not to be used

Upon completing the FAT and receiving the unit on-site, a SAT should be conducted. Even those that do have the FAT will undergo a SAT to assure that everything is intact and nothing was lost along the way in shipping. Certainly, those items shipped without a FAT will often have a SAT. Even if the vendor is across the street from the company, damage may be incurred during shipment. Instruments get bumped, joints may loosen, or parts may fall off or get lost if they were shipped separately. In any case, units undergoing a FAT should also have a SAT[b] to assure that all components are still in place and functional. These tests are also conducted via a written protocol. This protocol also needs to be reviewed and approved by the manufacturing company prior to starting testing.

Upon receipt of the unit the receiving (manufacturer) company verifies the unit as per the purchase order requirements. The manufacturing company then prepares and approves the SAT protocol for both small and large units (often the same basic tests as performed in the FAT). The SAT is used to show that the unit that has been received was not damaged during shipment and that all components are still intact. The SAT while similar to the FAT is usually a simpler test protocol just to assure the unit is intact and not damaged during shipment. The commissioning comes next.

So, what is a commissioning protocol?

---

[b] https://learnaboutgmp.com/good-validation-practices/the-difference-between-a-fat-and-a-sat-video/.

Commissioning[c]

Following the FAT/SAT portion of the equipment purchase and installation, the unit can be commissioned. Understanding the use and the how and why of commissioning is another critical step in setting up an effective equipment qualification program. Commissioning is "bring (something newly produced, such as a factory or machine) into working condition." By this definition, all equipment to be used in a pharmaceutical plant use should be commissioned, at least to some degree. Commissioning[d] is a ubiquitous operation that is very often overlooked even in our daily lives. For example, when we purchase a car, the dealer commissions the car for us. Here, for example, the dealer fills the gas tank, checks the windshield fluid, and checks tire pressure. Likewise, when a new piece of process equipment is purchased and installed, after the FAT/SAT, commissioning needs to be done to make the unit ready for use. According to industry standards, commissioning is a preplanned, documented, and managed approach to assure that the equipment is ready for use as intended. All major components need to be verified, flow rates need to be adjusted, temperatures need calibration, preventive maintenance may also have to be performed, etc.

Side Note

As with any item we purchase, whether an item purchased in a store or ordered from an on line vendor, the first thing anyone does is inspect the package. Any defect in the package may indicate a possible defect in the product. This is also true of pharmaceutical equipment. The next thing we usually do is to open the package, inspect the unit for damage and decide to accept it or return it to the vendor. This is easier for home items that pharmaceutical equipment, however, if there is evident damage the vendor is contacted and rectification of the issue is made.

The next step is to place the unit in place (kitchen shelf, night table, etc.). For pharmaceutical equipment it may be necessary to have made special provisions for the unit to be installed. This may include things like a thicker cement pad, a vibrations absorbing pad, a noise-reducing environment, or other specific requirements for the correct operation of the equipment.

---

[c] Commissioning and Qualification of Existing Facilities and Systems, J. Butterfield, R & D Magazine, 2005 (https://www.rdmag.com/article/2005/07/commissioning-and-qualification-existing-facilities-and-systems).

[d] ISPE Baseline Guide Vol 5, "Commissioning and Qualification" March 2001.

Following the placement of the unit into its proper location we are often anxious to start it up. While this may be possible for a toaster, or an alarm clock it is not so easy with a piece of pharmaceutical equipment. A forklift, crane, or other large piece of equipment is often needed to move or place a unit in its proper place. Care must be taken using these devices as well.

Now that the unit is in place, at home we try it out, in the pharmaceutical industry we need to do some further work. It needs to be fixed in place (except for portable units) according to the manufacturers specifications (i.e., distance from the wall, floor or ceiling, level, etc.) While it may be easy to refer to the installation instructions alone, or to have the machine manufacturer perform the installation this is not the accepted way of doing things. A protocol has to be written and executed.

This verification is accomplished with a commissioning protocol. The engineering group usually prepares the commissioning protocol since they are often the ones who are responsible for the installation of the unit. In some cases the company producing the equipment will install the unit according to the manufacturing company's requirements and their own specifications. This protocol while similar to the IQ and OQ protocols discussed in Chapter 8 does have some major differences (see Table 2). First of all, as defined, it is intended to get the equipment ready for use as compared to testing it to be sure it meets the required specifications.[e] That means changes can be made without going through the change control procedures (note: is some cases the quality unit does want to sign the protocol, thus making it a GMP document and thus may be subject to the change control program). The reason to keep this part of the qualification program as a separate item is to allow the engineers, the operation staff, or the vendor to make the necessary changes, according to predetermined testing, following a written set of procedures so that all changes or modifications that are made to the unit are correctly recorded and these changes will be incorporated and verified in the IQ and/or OQ protocol. The commissioning protocol can be as simple as a checklist (e.g., unit has two blades; motor is 2 HP) or more complex as to having defined specifications to be met (e.g., flow rates and RPM requirements).

Some examples of commissioning changes can be seen in Table 3.

---

[e] Commissioning—Key to Project Success, D. Owings, Pharmaceutical Manufacturing, Sep./Oct. 2002, 22:5.

Table 2 Commissioning versus qualification

Commissioning

- Check sheet/protocol
- Engineering/construction
- Corrections made as necessary
- Start-up activity
- Not necessarily a GMP document
- Changes made need to be documented
- Purpose is to get equipment ready for use

Qualification

- A GMP activity
- Specified versus actual
- Predetermined acceptance criteria
- Preapproval of the protocol is needed
- Purpose is to prove usability for a specific function
- Required if there is any product contact
- Summary report needed
- More detailed

Table 3 Examples of some commissioning steps

- Adjusting the rate of ozone flowing in a purified water system
- Changing a stuck gauge for a comparable working one
- Changing a gauge to a more sensitive scale (i.e., the original gauge reads from 0 to 100 psi, but the pressure needed for the system only goes to 25 psi, so a gauge reading from 0 to 50 psi is more appropriate).
- I/O checks (loop checks)
- Verifying polarity of electric outlet
- Bumping the pump (check for rotation and speed)
- Leveling the unit
- Verifying distance from wall, floor, and ceiling
- Verifying utility connections
- Checking (adjusting as needed)
  - Flow rate(s)
  - Pressure(s)
  - Temperature(s)
  - Speed(s)

The commissioning protocol needs to check the operation and range of the gauges, flows, temperatures, etc. based on the process information produced during the development stage for the process. All changes made during the execution of the commissioning protocol are to be carefully documented and approved by the corresponding authority. This means that a change in a valve size needs engineering approval while a change to flow rate of the product would require approval by the production or operation team.

Using commissioning data

While getting the equipment ready for use is the main purpose of commissioning, there is another advantage to having a well-defined, well-documented commissioning program in place. This advantage is that some, if not all, of the commissioning tests may be used to support or replace testing that would have to be tested in the IQ or OQ. This is at the discretion of the quality unit. For example:

- A pump is turned on during commissioning (bumped) to check direction and possibly speed of rotation. This would not have to be repeated in the OQ if QU approves. This may also confirm electric polarity for the pump, and that is an IQ function.
- The flow of ozone during the sanitization cycle of a water system was adjusted to the level recommended by the vendor during commissioning (it was received set at lower setting during shipping). The correct flow is acknowledged in the commissioning protocol and would not have to be reverified in the OQ, again with approval of QU.
- I/O checks performed during installation can be used for not only the commissioning part of the installation but also part of the IQ, again with QU approval and preapproved I/O checklist.

A question often arises, "what if a component is not in place during the commissioning?" Can IQ and/or OQ be started? Here the simple answer is "yes" at the discretion of the quality unit. However, any test that would include the missing component cannot be performed until the component is in place. No deviation need be recorded at this time since the testing has not been started or completed. Once the missing component is installed, the testing can be completed. If there is a problem encountered at this time, a deviation or further investigation needs to be performed. Remember, this is still not a GMP document, and change control does not apply (unless as required by the quality unit).

Decommissioning[f]

At the end of the unit's life cycle—that is, its useful life—or the end of its need for a particular process, the unit needs to be decommissioned prior

[f] ISPE, Good practice Guide: Decommissioning of Pharmaceutical Equipment and Facilities, 2014.

to removal from the production line. As per the definition, decommissioning is a "planned shutdown or removal of a building, equipment, plant, etc. from operation or usage."

Decommissioning is a process of getting the equipment that has been used for a pharmaceutical process ready to be taken off-line, repurposed, sold, or discarded. Each of these scenarios has their own approach and needs. The process may have changed, the process may have been scaled up under the FDA guidance document Scale-up and Post-Approval Change—IR[g] (SUPAC-IR) or other means, or the process may have been discontinued. Just as when the equipment was new and just being installed, the equipment needs to be made ready for sale or destruction. It needs to be made safe for others who may purchase it or for those disposing of the unit.

As always a decommissioning protocol needs to be prepared, reviewed, and approved. Again, as in the commissioning protocol, this can be a simple checklist or more complicated to include cleaning instructions and verification and full disassembly. Table 4 lists some of the items that should be considered when planning a decommissioning.

Table 4 Decommissioning considerations

1. Product(s) used in the unit
2. Cleaning agent(s) used
3. Safety check
   a. Interlocks
   b. Lubricants—in place, removal
   c. Metal fatigue—cracking, etc.
   d. HASOP analysis
4. Depending on disposition
   a. Operational
   b. D rated as necessary
5. Notification to regulatory agencies
6. Notification to all end users
7. Building considerations—removal from the building/area of use
   a. Size—disassembly
   b. Storage
   c. Clean up

---

[g] FDA Guidance for Industry: SUPAC-IR Immediate Release Solid Oral Dosage Forms, Scale—Up and Post-approval Changes: Chemistry, Manufacturing, and Controls, In Vitro Dissolution Testing, In Vivo Bioequivalence Documentation, Guidance, November 1995.

A machine that has been correctly decommissioned can be sold or scrapped as needed by the company. The closeout document or decommissioning report should include items such as listed in Table 4. When the decommissioning program is complete, the unit may be safely sold and used or discarded. In some cases the FDA or other regulatory agency may need to be notified of the decommissioning. This is especially true if the unit is to be replaced by another piece of equipment.

Equipment qualification protocols

Previous chapters have guided us to the point of preparing the equipment qualification protocol(s). The purpose of the equipment qualification protocol(s) is to demonstrate to the users/owners and the regulatory agencies that the equipment ordered (specified), received is correct and installed correctly (premanufacture requirements) and that it will function as intended for the intended purpose of the product(s). Chapter 6 discussed the general approach to preparing a protocol. Chapter 7 discussed the process of commissioning the equipment. Now, the equipment needs to have documentation that "proves" it is ready for the actual operation. This demonstration will show the functionality and stability of the equipment. The FDA bases acceptance of a unit on establishing a risk profile[a] and on a good scientific approach. But as already stated, equipment qualification is primarily needed to assure the manufacturer that the correct unit is in place and will work as needed for the product and that the product(s) produced will be of the highest quality and reproducibly manufactured.

For the purposes of equipment qualification in addition to the commissioning protocol (Chapter 7), there are three major qualification protocols that are needed to be prepared.[b]

These are the following:
- Installation qualification—IQ—all important physical characteristics needed for operation.
- Operational qualification—OQ—all (full range) operating parameters of the equipment.
- Performance qualification—PQ—duration testing and compliance to specified operating parameters for the product(s) or a combination of units that will function together, for example, a filling–packaging line.

Each of these protocols can be stand-alone documents or combined (e.g., IOQ). In every case, they need to be prepared *specifically* for the unit(s) being qualified. The IQ and OQ may also be combined into a document called the

---

[a]FDA, Pharmaceutical CGMPS for the 21st Century—A Risk-Based Approach, FDA, Sept. 2004.
[b]"What are IQ, OQ, and PQ? Why are they needed in the Pharmaceutical Industry?" Wellspring Pharma Services, May 15, 2014.

Equipment Qualification in the Pharmaceutical Industry
https://doi.org/10.1016/B978-0-12-817568-2.00008-7

Table 1 Qualification considerations

- Product contact
    - Direct contact
        - Equipment directly touches the product or an ingredient/component
        - Material of construction needs to be verified for product contact surfaces only
    - Indirect contact
        - May have product contact if a leak or breach was to occur
        - May be incidental contact
    - No contact
        - There is no contact by the equipment or any of its components with the product or any or its components
- Criticality
- Safety—product and personnel
- System suitability
- Environmental conditions

IOQ or EQ (equipment qualification). Sometimes all three are combined; however, the PQ is often a stand-alone document since it requires longer testing and often requires a combination of equipment to demonstrate effectiveness for the process range and conditions.

After collecting the relevant data on the equipment (drawings, manuals, etc.), a risk analysis on the equipment as related to the process (based on good science and product requirements) needs to be completed. Remember, in general, the greater the possibility of product/component contact, the greater amount of qualification needed. Examples of items to consider for the risk analysis are (but not limited to) seen in Table 1.

Product contact

Contact of the product with the surface of the equipment is certainly a major criterion in determining the extent of the qualification process. Surfaces that directly touch the product (this may even include the air in the room or other gases) need to have a full analysis, testing, and documentation to demonstrate (or prove) that the material does not affect or alter the product in any way.[c] In situations where the contact is indirect or incidental (e.g., this may be room air and compressed air in pneumatic valves), the protocol needs to prove that if it was to contact the product or drug substance, the

[c]FDA, 21 CFR 211.65.

product would not be adversely affected. Thus, materials that may possibly have contact with the product should be food-grade material (wherever possible). For surfaces not coming in contact with the product, for example, a cooling tower, commissioning may be the only qualification required.

Criticality

This relates to both the process itself and the equipment being used. Have the key process parameters (KPPs) and critical process parameters (CPPs) been identified? Is the unit involved with a KPP or a CPP? Before preparing a protocol to test the installation or operation of a unit, it is important to know what the user expects from the unit. This leads to the determination of the criticality of the unit for the process. It will be found that some pieces of equipment are "placeholders" in the process, that is, holding material until the next addition or process step is to be completed, while others are so important that any change in the equipment will be detrimental to the process. For example, a filling machine is critical to the process as well as meeting key parameters. Based on the risk management approach currently in use, the higher the criticality of the unit, the more extensive testing and documentation need to be completed.

Safety

While safety is not directly a CGMP requirement, determination of this factor in preparing the qualification protocol certainly needs to be considered. Safety concerns include both the safety to the product (this is CGMP) and safety to the workers. Safety items, for example, interlocking mechanisms, auto-shutoff valves, or switches, need to be identified and documented in the IQ, tested in the OQ, and even stressed in the PQ. While these systems do not directly affect the production of the product, they are an integral part of the operation and protect not only the operators but also the product from adverse conditions. As an example, an access door to the filling heads needs to be closed during operation, and the machine needs to shut off all operation if the door is opened during production. The reason for this is twofold: First is the safety to the product and personnel from moving parts, and second is assuring the continuation of the correct air flow in the unit again protecting the product from outside particles or influence.

System suitability

In documenting system suitability, the company needs to be assured that the correct equipment has been selected for its intended purpose. As always, the users must be asked the precise use of the unit prior to ordering the unit and upon inspecting it on its arrival at the site. An example of this would be if you are going to separate molecules based on their ionic charges, the chromatography column should be an ion exchange column not a size exclusion column. This is to be determined during the development stage for the process.[d] In addition, the equipment needs to be able to stand up the demands of the manufacturing process. Here for example, can it withstand operation at 80% on and 20% off cycles? Does the product become "sticky" and cling to the surface of the equipment requiring frequent cleanouts?

Some units may come with more functions than needed for a given process. As an example, a spectrophotometer may have one or more USB ports for data storage or transfer. However, if the company is not going to use these ports, they need to be closed and marked "NOT IN USE" so that accidental use is not possible. Units that have additional functionality than required need only to qualify the required functions after determination that the unused functions do not adversely affect the results of the equipment.

Environmental conditions

An often-overlooked aspect of protocol development is the state of the environment in which the equipment is located. There are two aspects of this parameter. The first is that the product or drug substance may be sensitive to humidity, heat, light, oxygen, etc. The second part is that the equipment needs to be able to function under the room conditions in which it will be used. As an example, computer servers (or controllers) tend to generate heat as they operate. Thus, if the temperature in the room where they are located gets too hot, they may fail to operate correctly; adding alarms will notify the users of this problem. Adding additional cooling will help alleviate or prevent a problem from occurring.

---

[d]Ostrove, S., How to Validate a Pharmaceutical Process. Academic Press, 2016.

Before discussing each of the qualification protocols in more depth, there are certain basic criteria or conditions that need to be met:

- As discussed earlier, the first of these is that each protocol should represent a "stand-alone system." An example of a stand-alone system is a refrigerator or a dry-heat oven. These have many internal components that are critical to their operation but are not necessarily visible from the outside yet are all needed to assure proper operation of the refrigerator. This is why the P&ID is so important:
    - A pseudo-stand-alone system would be a tank. While it is true that a tank will hold liquid without the aid of anything external, it cannot fill itself nor mix the ingredients by itself. Thus the pump, the agitator, the piping, and the tank would constitute a stand-alone system.
- The second consideration is that only those components that have to do with the actual operation of the unit for its specific purpose need to be qualified (or they have direct product contact). For example, the screws or rivets holding the nameplate to the unit do not have to be included in the protocol—they do not affect operation of the unit (unless they protrude into the product contact area).
- The third item is to understand the function of the unit. For this, one has to know which of the functions of the unit to be used. As before, if the unit has 10 functions and only 5 will be used for the current operation, only the 5 functions needed are to be qualified. However, one must be sure that none of the other five (the ones not being qualified) interfere or affect the operation of the five that are to be used. Also, as noted earlier, it is preferable to mark the unused functions as "out of service" (if they are physical entities available on the outside of the unit) or not in use if possible. Note that if they can't be marked or shut off, the unused functions may be inadvertently used, so it is often a good idea to qualify all functions so that any can be used at a later time or if inadvertently used will not result in a deviation investigation.
- A fourth step is to prepare a prospective protocol (Chapter 6). This is one that has predetermined acceptance criteria that need to be met. In some limited cases a concurrent qualification may be allowed, but the prospective approach is still needed. Qualifying a process unit by retrospective analysis, that is, saying it has worked for X number of runs, is not an acceptable approach for qualification today.

To fully understand the use of each of the protocol types, let's further explore their intent and why they are needed and the components of each protocol. Don't forget that all testing is to be performed against the user requirements and not necessarily the design requirements.

Protocols[e]
Installation qualification

The IQ protocol is used to document all of the "important" physical characteristics of the equipment. Note here the word *important*. Only those physical characteristics or components that are needed for the operation of the unit or that have a direct or indirect impact on the product preparation need to be included in the protocol. This includes the material of construction in contact with the product, moving parts allowing the unit to function, or other parts of the equipment that impact its operation (e.g., motors, impellers, pumps, and valves). Here, for example, if a tank is jacketed so as to maintain a given temperature, the material of construction of the inner lining (contact with the product) needs to be identified (material of construction—MOC), whereas the material of construction of the jacket (outside the tank walls) that is critical to the operation and that does not come into contact with the product (incidental or possible contact) does not necessarily need to be listed (but it usually is). It does need to be included in the protocol as a functional piece of the equipment since it is an integral part of the process. On the other hand, if the jacketed tank is being used but there is no heating or cooling function needed or used, then the jacket would necessarily be mentioned as existing but not "qualified" in the protocol.

Table 2 lists the general items (included but not limited to) to be considered for or verified in an IQ protocol (an example of a page from an IQ can be found in the Appendix). The protocol is often divided into four columns as shown in Fig. 1. A fifth column may be added for comments. Note: for existing equipment, the column for "as specified" is often omitted.

Items such as the MOC of product contact surfaces, sizes of the chamber that holds the process materials during production, or the sizes of ports used

[e]ISPE, Baseline Guide, Vol 5, Commissioning and Qualification, March 2001.

Table 2 General considerations of the IQ protocol.

- Verify installation that is as specified by the manufacturer and the operating company
- Insert a brief description of the operational function
- Verify associated utilities that are commissioned or qualified prior to executing the IQ
- Verify that all alarms, gauges, and other visual displays are listed
- Confirm that the software is correct (version, etc.)
- Identify and verify that serial numbers, make, model, etc. are identified[a] of all components that are part of the unit's operation
- Review calibration[b] certificates for all instruments
- Verify that the environmental conditions are acceptable for the unit's operation
- Verify the documentation provided
- Verify capacity and other physical properties
- Identifiable components present
- Drawings and documents are up to date (e.g., as built)
- Weld and pressure test reports are present
- Lubricant/consumable list
- Field identification has been performed and verified from the manual(s)

[a]21 CFR 821.30.
[b]21 CFR 210.

Item	As specified	As found	How verified	Comments
Manufacturer	XYZ company			
Make	The best			
Model	Best #1			
Material of Construction	316 SS			
Serial number				

Fig. 1 Simple layout of an IQ page.

to add or remove material(s) (or samples) are examples of IQ parameters that are common to all IQ protocols and are needed to be included. Table 3 lists (again includes but not limited to) just some of the characteristics needed in all IQ protocols.

Table 3 Common items for all IQs

General characteristic	Specific characteristic	Comments
Material of construction	All product contact surfaces	21 CFR 211.65
Ports (in/out)	Ports, types (connectors if any)	Number, location, internal diameter
Sizes, capacity	Any opening, vessel height/width/ diameter	
Distance from floor/wall/ ceiling		21 CFR 211.63 and 211.65
Type of mounting	Leg types, wall mounts	Depends on room classification
Electric	Voltage/amps/hertz	Grounding type
Unit identifications	Tag no.	21 CFR 211.105
Weld reports		
Major components	Agitators, controls	Controls may be included in computer section
Utilities and connections		
Direction of rotation	Agitators, pumps	
Make/model/ ser. no.		
Pressure tests		
Utility connections		Do the utilities need qualification prior to the equipment's qualification?

Operational qualification

The operational qualification protocol should be designed to test the actual operation of the unit, that is, the design specifications. Again, as in the IQ (expected results), there should be predetermined results or acceptance criteria for each test. Each criterion should be quantifiable (there may be some exceptions) rather than just a pass/fail. The unit should be tested over its full operating range so as to minimize retesting in the future if the need for other speeds, temperatures, etc. is needed. In some instances, a limited operational test may be performed (e.g., over a limited range) to save time (at the time of qualification). Table 4 lists the general considerations of OQ protocols, while Table 5 lists some of the items usually found in an OQ protocol (specific to the actual function of the unit).

Table 4 The considerations for the OQ[a]

- Part 11 if necessary
- Full operational range
- All control operation
- Calibration
- Flow of materials
- Test design versus output
- Verification of all loop installations/verification
- Testing of alarms
- Testing of interlocks
- Verification of the functionality
- Challenge of software (where possible)
- Power loss recovery
- Testing of all interfaces between
- Testing for electromagnetic interference and compatibility

[a]Includes but not limited to.

Table 5 Examples of OQ items

- Full range of operation
- System output versus design
  - Product flow
  - Motor amperage
  - Speed
    - Direction of operation
    - Control
- Calibration of system instruments
- Calibration of test instruments (before and after each test)
- Controls
  - Alarm and interlock operation
  - Ranges
  - Function
- Utility pressures and flows
- System SOPs available
- System recovery after power failure
- Computer function/Part 11 compliance
  - I/O loop checks
  - Password access
  - Data storage security/retrieval
  - System challenges
- Cleaning verification
- Emergency power operation (what happens after a power failure)
- Test FULL operating range of the equipment
- System suitability test
  - Functions for intended purpose
  - Functions as designed (user/functional specifications)
- Controls

As in all good scientific experiments, each OQ test should have one variable and thus one acceptance criteria that is measurable.

The layout for each test script is usually the following:
- Test name
- Supplies needed
- Procedure
- Results (acceptance criteria shown)
- Conclusions (pass/fail)

An example of an OQ page can be seen in the Appendix examples.

Performance qualification

The IQ and OQ have already demonstrated that the unit can operate as expected (i.e., requested by the users—user requirements; operate as expected by the manufacturer and process engineering group) and that all major components are present to affect the operation. The PQ is used as necessary to demonstrate that the unit will be able to function within the production range for the period of time necessary to produce a stable, consistent product. For example, a 5000-gal bioreactor was said to be controlled to ±2°C. The OQ showed that the controller could regulate temperatures to ±1°C. The question that was asked is, "is it the controller that will be controlled to ±2°C specification or will the entire 5000-gal reactor be controlled to that specification for the time needed for the reaction to be completed?" (Answer: it was the controller.)

Not all units require a PQ protocol (checking with the USP is often helpful). As an example, a pump and tank combination where no activity is occurring in the tank and the pump is used only to pump the liquid into the tank would not require a PQ. That is, the tank that is being used for holding purposes only does not require a PQ. This is quite different from a similar configuration where the liquid is being heated or cooled or other ingredients are being added. In that case the PQ would be required (e.g., dwell time at temperature and mixing speeds). Another example would be an autoclave where temperature mapping of the load configuration(s) needs to be included in the PQ. The PQ protocol is designed to demonstrate that the unit can operate within the desired range of operation for the length of time needed for the operation to be correctly executed. In addition, it needs to demonstrate that it can and does function as part of the production path (e.g., a filler needs to operate at the same rate of speed over the entire fill operation and also the same speed as the feeder/hopper and the conveyer following to the packaging machine) (Table 6).

Table 6 PQ parameters—process functionality

- Duration of function—process ranges
- Consistency of operation
- Microorganism count
- Types of operations (mixing, blending, and granulation)
- Pyrogen level
- Chemical purity
- Particle size
- Content uniformity

An example of a PQ page can be seen in the example part of the Appendix.

Protocol review

As discussed in Chapter 6, all protocols need to be reviewed by the appropriate groups that have a stake in the unit operations (e.g., engineering, operations, metrology, safety, and quality). Quality always signs last so as to assure that all corporate and compliance items are met. Remember, all protocols need to be approved BEFORE they are executed and again AFTER they are executed. Some companies save the executed (post) review for the final report. This leave the protocol unreviewed for a longer period of time making investigations more difficult. Most sign the pre- and postapproval pages for the protocol and then prepare the final report (Chapter 11) covering the IQ/OQ and/or PQ.

CHAPTER NINE

Equipment checklists

The lists presented in this chapter are not all-inclusive. Each table is separated by a specific piece of operation or support equipment. The tables include some of the most common items to be tested. However, it does not take into account items that may have been addressed in the risk management program (Chapters 2 and 3), also known as the quality risk management (QRM),[a] or by commissioning alone (Chapter 7). However, it provides a guideline for the preparation of a full qualification protocol. There may be other items that need to be included not on this list and certainly items that do not need to be included in every qualification protocol. All items and test will depend on the actual piece of equipment and its intended use. The specialist needs to refer to the operation manual and the maintenance manual as well as the risk analysis to be assured that all necessary components are addressed and tested properly.

It is important to remember that protocols should be prepared as "stand-alone units" (Chapter 6); thus items such as motors and tanks are usually not qualified independently but are included as part of a more inclusive system protocol covering all parts. Another item for consideration is the extent of computer control. Is the unit controlled by a microchip or a fully functioning computer system? The more independent the computer control, the more likely a separate protocol will be required (Chapter 5).

It is entirely up to the specialist as to what is included as based on the risk management program already performed. There are overlaps and similarities between units, and units are generally combined (e.g., pumps and tanks and agitators). It is critical that each piece of equipment or equipment system be considered for its specific design and function. Another point to consider is that all items qualified or listed in the IQ need to be tested in the OQ and/or PQ.

Be sure to consider the list for all IQs and OQs in addition to the specific listings in the tables later. When considering this list, keep in mind that

[a] FDA Guidance for Industry Quality Risk Management, June 2006.

Equipment Qualification in the Pharmaceutical Industry
https://doi.org/10.1016/B978-0-12-817568-2.00009-9

commissioning has been or should have been completed previously. Items that were included in commissioning, as pointed out in Chapter 7, do not need to be retested unless the quality unit requires this. Thus, following the risk-based approach may minimize some of the tests proposed in these lists. As discussed in Chapter 10 at the start of protocol execution, the P&ID will be "walked" to assure all components are in place as specified so that reconfirmation of some items will not be necessary.

As an additional word of caution, more is not necessarily better. That is, a larger protocol is not necessarily a better protocol. The protocol should cover only those items necessary for the functioning of the unit (this could be for multiple products or a single product).

The following lists for the various pieces of process equipment are representative of the most common used in the industry. NOTE: in the tables later, IQ indicates primarily an IQ function to be verified; OQ indicates an operational testing for that function is needed (as well as verifying any IQ functions such as lights turning on, etc.; PQ indicates a performance functions that needs to be tested. This may be either alone or in conjunction with other pieces of equipment. Where items are marked IQ/OQ, it means that the functions may overlap such as verifying capacity of a tank and that it holds the correct amount of liquid.

The IQ will usually compare the "specified" with the "as found," while the OQ will test unit functionality. In some cases, for example, serial number or asset number, only the as-found is needed since it is being used primarily for identification purposes.

IQ items for all units

Y/N	IQ/OQ/PQ	Item
☐	IQ	Material of construction
☐	IQ	Manufacturer
☐	IQ	Model
☐	IQ	Serial number
☐	IQ	Level (horizontal/vertical)
☐	IQ	Surface finish—external
☐	IQ	Surface finish—wetted parts
☐	IQ	Tag number
☐	IQ	Type of mounting
☐	IQ	Controls (on/off, light indicators, speed, etc.)
☐	IQ	Location/setup (floor/ceiling/walls)
☐	IQ	Utility connections—correct and tight and listed
☐	IQ	ALL MAJOR COMPONENTS

OQ items for all units

Y/N	IQ/OQ/PQ	Item
☐	OQ	Controls work
☐	OQ	Full operation range (temp/speed)
☐	OQ	All items listed in the IQ (controls, lights, etc.)
☐	OQ	Output versus design functions

Motors

Y/N	IQ/OQ/PQ	Item
☐	IQ	Volts/phase/hertz
☐	IQ	Enclosure type
☐	IQ	Horse power
☐	IQ	Rated current drain
☐	IQ	Listed speed/range (RPM)
☐	IQ	Listed direction of rotation
☐	IQ	Shaft diameter/type[a]
☐	IQ	Frame size
☐	IQ	Variable/reversible
☐	IQ	Seal types—MOC
☐	IQ	Lubricants
☐	IQ	Differential pressure head (max/min)
☐	IQ	Type (two stroke, etc.)
☐	OQ	Speed control (max/min)
☐	OQ	Controls function correctly
☐	OQ	Flow rate (fill or empty)
☐	PQ	Speed consistency
☐	PQ	Flow consistency
☐	PQ	Pressure consistency

[a]Rarely needed but may apply for assuring centering of the shaft.

Pumps

Y/N	IQ/OQ/PQ	Item
☐	IQ	Volts/phase/hertz
☐	IQ	Enclosure type
☐	IQ	Horsepower
☐	IQ	Rated current drain
☐	IQ	Listed speed/range (RPM)
☐	IQ	Listed direction of rotation
☐	IQ	Shaft diameter/type
☐	IQ	Frame size
☐	IQ	Variable/reversible
☐	IQ	Seals (types/MOC)
☐	IQ	Lubricants

Y/N	IQ/OQ/PQ	Item
☐	IQ	Ports/fittings/type/number
☐	IQ	Differential pressure head (max/min)
☐	IQ	Type (centrifugal/peristaltic/reciprocating/other)
☐	IQ	Impeller type
☐	IQ	Max/min flow (range)
☐	OQ	Speed control (max/min)
☐	OQ	Pressure control
☐	OQ	Pressure—max/min
☐	OQ	Controls function correctly
☐	OQ	Flow rate (fill or empty)
☐	PQ	Speed consistency
☐	PQ	Flow consistency
☐	PQ	Pressure consistency

Vessels/tanks/totes[a]

Y/N	IQ/OQ/PQ	Item
☐	IQ	Number of ports/connections[a]
☐	IQ	Type of ports/connections[a]
☐	IQ	Size/capacity
☐	IQ	Impeller (type/size)
☐	IQ	Jacketed (Y/N)
☐	IQ	Number of valves—types
☐	IQ	Number of instruments
☐	IQ	Seal type (and MOC)
☐	IQ	Type of agitator
☐	IQ	Location of agitator (top/bottom mount)
☐	IQ	Design pressure (ASTM Rating 0)
☐	IQ	Design temperature
☐	IQ	Jacket temperature range
☐	IQ	ANSI/ASTM rating
☐	OQ	Temperature ramp up/ramp down)
☐	OQ	Holds liquid (no leaks)
☐	PQ	Temperature stability

[a]Many IQ items may be verified on the P&ID walk-through.

Agitators

Y/N	IQ/OQ/PQ	Item
☐	IQ	Type
☐	IQ	Location
☐	IQ	Number of impellers/number of blades
☐	IQ	Impeller size
☐	IQ	Impeller speed range (max/min)
☐	IQ	Seal type
☐	IQ	Number of ports/connections
☐	IQ	Type of connections

Y/N	IQ/OQ/PQ	Item
☐	IQ	Lubricant
☐	IQ	Direction of rotation
☐	IQ	Impeller pitch
☐	OQ	Speed range
☐	OQ	Direction of rotation
☐	PQ	Consistency of operation
☐	PQ	Stability of rotation (centered)

Valves/instruments

Y/N	IQ/OQ/PQ	Item
☐	IQ	Type (manual/pneumatic/electric/other)
☐	IQ	Volts/phase
☐	IQ	Design pressure
☐	IQ	Number of ports (in versus out)
☐	IQ	Type of connection/ports
☐	IQ	Nominal size—piping
☐	IQ	Function
☐	IQ	Manual/automatic
☐	IQ	Design temperature/pressure—range
☐	OQ	I/O connection
☐	OQ	Open ¼, ½, ¾, full
☐	OQ	Speed of opening or closing

Heat exchangers

Y/N	IQ/OQ/PQ	Item
☐	IQ	Type
☐	IQ	Surface area
☐	IQ	Design temperature
☐	IQ	Design pressure
☐	IQ	Heat transfer fluid
☐	IQ	Number of ports/connections
☐	IQ	Type of connections
☐	OQ	Heat exchange rate
☐	PQ	Functions for the required time

Autoclaves

Y/N	IQ/OQ/PQ	Item
☐	IQ	WFI source
☐	IQ	Validation port
☐	IQ	Controls
☐	IQ	Chamber size
☐	IQ	Door configuration—lock mechanism

☐	OQ	Empty chamber temperature map[a]
☐	OQ	Pressure hold test
☐	OQ	Functional test of cycles
☐	OQ	Ramp-up time, ramp-down time
☐	OQ	Steam pressure/quality
☐	OQ	Lock function
☐	PQ	Load configuration test(s)
☐	PQ	Biotest strips kill (spore reduction map)/F_0

[a]This will need to be repeated annually to assure that the cold and hot spots are the same.

Filters

Y/N	IQ/OQ/PQ	Item
☐	IQ	Type (nonshedding)
☐	IQ	Surface area/capacity
☐	IQ	Type of connections
☐	IQ	Design pressure/temperature
☐	IQ	Number of ports/connections
☐	OQ	Pressure drop (max/min)
☐	OQ	Nominal filtration rate
☐	OQ	Bubble point (water or product)

Dryers

Y/N	IQ/OQ/PQ	Item
☐	IQ	Type
☐	IQ	Size/capacity
☐	IQ	Fan(s)
☐	IQ	Design pressure
☐	IQ	Number/type of instruments
☐	IQ	Door gasket/seals
☐	IQ	Number of shelves
☐	IQ	Dust collector—type
☐	OQ	Heat-up time/cooldown time
☐	OQ	Pressure max
☐	OQ	Dust collector vacuum
☐	OQ	Empty chamber mapping[a]
☐	PQ	Load configuration mapping

[a]This will need to be repeated annually to assure that the cold and hot spots are the same.

Blenders/mixers

Y/N	IQ/OQ/PQ	Item
☐	IQ	Type
☐	IQ	Size/capacity
☐	IQ	Impeller/blade type/pitch
☐	IQ	Design pressure

Y/N	IQ/OQ/PQ	Item
☐	IQ	Impeller/blade rotation direction
☐	IQ	Number of ports/connections
☐	IQ	Type of connections
☐	IQ	Jacketed (temperature range)
☐	IQ	Lubricant
☐	IQ	Impeller/blade speed range
☐	IQ	Number of valves
☐	IQ	Number/type of instruments
☐	OQ	Impeller/blade rotation direction
☐	OQ	Impeller/blade speed range
☐	OQ	Max load
☐	OQ	Rotation speed
☐	PQ	Depends on materials in unit

Fillers

Y/N	IQ/OQ/PQ	Item
☐	IQ	Number of fill heads (solid or liquid)
☐	IQ	Hopper volume
☐	IQ	Controls
☐	OQ	Fill speed
☐	OQ	Conveyor belt speed
☐	OQ	Rate of fill
☐	OQ	Shape of tablet, etc.
☐	PQ	Fill material

Lyophilizers

Y/N	IQ/OQ/PQ	Item
☐	IQ/OQ	Size/capacity
☐	IQ/OQ	Vacuum (max)
☐	IQ/OQ	Temp pull-down rate
☐	IQ	Temperature specs
☐	IQ/OQ	Door seals
☐	IQ	Shelve type
☐	OQ	Shelve operation
☐	OQ	Alarms/interlocks
☐	OQ	Time
☐	OQ	Cooldown rate
☐	OQ	Stopper placement
☐	OQ	Temperature map
☐	PQ	Load configuration
☐	PQ	Cake configuration
☐	PQ	Cake reconstitution

Accumulator table/belts

Y/N	IQ/OQ/PQ	Item
☐	IQ/OQ	Speed
☐	IQ/OQ	Direction of rotation
☐	IQ/OQ	Capacity

Vial/bottle washer

Y/N	IQ/OQ/PQ	Item
☐	IQ/OQ	Blowout type
☐	IQ/OQ	Wash type
☐	IQ/OQ	Drying (type/rate)

Capper

Y/N	IQ/OQ/PQ	Item
☐	IQ	Capacity
☐	IQ	Cap size (min–max)
☐	IQ/OQ	Speed
☐	IQ/OQ	Torque

Induction sealer

Y/N	IQ/OQ/PQ	Item
☐	IQ	Height
☐	IQ	Dimensions
☐	IQ/OQ	Temperature (mapping of tunnel required)
☐	IQ/OQ	Speed range
☐	PQ	Temperature at product level

Rabs/isolators

Y/N	IQ/OQ/PQ	Item
☐	IQ	Ports (number–type)
☐	IQ	Type
☐	IQ/OQ	Seals
☐	IQ/OQ	Pressure
☐	IQ/OQ	Openings (getting items in and out)
☐	PQ	Air quality
☐	OQ	Interlock(s)

Rooms

Y/N	IQ/OQ/PQ	Item
☐	IQ	Type
☐	IQ	Size/capacity
☐	IQ	Classification
☐	IQ	Floor–wall–ceiling material
☐	IQ	Vibration free
☐	IQ	Windows/door (seals)
☐	OQ	Pressure differential
☐	OQ	Correct lighting
☐	OQ	Room pressurization
☐	IQ/OQ	Lighting
☐	IQ/OQ	Vibration free
☐	IQ/OQ	Windows/door seals

Computer components[a]

Y/N	IQ/OQ/PQ	Item
☐	IQ	Type—input means (human machine interface—I IMI)
☐	IQ	Power limits
☐	IQ	Temperature limits
☐	IQ	Ground connection tight
☐	OQ	Emergency power
☐	OQ	Functional testing
☐	OQ	Radio-frequency interference (RFI)
☐	OQ	Electromagnetic interference (EMI)

[a]Only when a full CSV is determined not to be required.

Cartoner

Y/N	IQ/OQ/PQ	Item
☐	IQ/OQ	Unfolder
☐	IQ/OQ	Packer
☐	IQ/OQ	Checkweigher
☐	IQ/OQ	Sealer
☐	IQ/OQ	Labeler

Chromatography systems

Y/N	IQ/OQ/PQ	Item
☐	IQ	Column dimensions (HxW)
☐	IQ	Resin composition
☐	IQ	Retainer ring composition
☐	IQ	Screen composition
☐	IQ	Detector (type-range)

☐	IQ/OQ	Pressure
☐	OQ	Flow rate
☐	OQ	Gradient composition
☐	OQ	Detector function
☐	OQ	Temperature control

CHAPTER TEN

Protocol execution

Once the protocol has been written, reviewed, and approved, the next step is to prepare for the execution of the protocol. The person assigned to execute the protocol should review the document, or a copy, prior to starting any field work. This will familiarize them with the testing to be performed, the test materials needed, and/or the items to be verified (as to being in place, correctly installed, and correct in all physical specifications).

As stated in Chapters 6 and 8 (General Protocol Preparation and Equipment Qualification Protocols), each protocol has a specific function. The IQ assures that all major or important physical components are present. The OQ assures that the unit will function over its full operating range. And the PQ proves that the unit will function consistently at the required speed, direction, temperature, etc. along with associated equipment so that the process can proceed correctly.

One of the first questions asked is, "can the IQ/OQ/PQ protocol testing be combined?" The simple answer is *yes*. However, there are some limitations to do this. As seen in Chapter 6, the protocols (usually IQ and OQ) can be combined into a single document and thus be executed as a single document. In addition, the quality unit needs to approve the combination and the ability to do linked testing.

The following is a simple example of why and how combining execution of the IQ and OQ makes sense. If the IQ says to identify valve 1 and the unit needs to be opened to see valve 1 and the OQ says to turn off valve 1, it probably would not make sense to open the machine and locate valve 1, close it up, and complete the IQ and then reopen the machine, locate valve 1, and turn it off during the OQ test. Another reason for reviewing the protocol prior to its execution is to familiarize the operator with the tests to be performed and the tools that will be needed. In addition, if an electrician or plumber is needed to perform a specific test or if a special piece of test equipment is needed, it would be known before starting the execution, and they would be available, and no time would be lost.

Yet another example of where the IQ and OQ testing were combined was with a high-speed granulator that was received missing one of the granulation blades. The quality unit approved combining IQ and OQ testing that did not include the missing blade. Once the blade was received and installed and confirmed installed in the IQ, completion of OQ testing was possible. In all cases the execution of the IQ must be completed (reviewed and approved and all deviations addressed) prior to the completion and approval of the OQ or PQ. Likewise the OQ needs to be approved prior to the PQ being signed and approved.

Prioritization[a]

Before starting any equipment qualification execution program (assuming more than one piece of equipment is to be qualified), it is best to prioritize of the order in which the equipment will undergo qualification. This is particularly true when planning the execution of the PQ protocols. Just as the protocols are generally prepared in the order in which they will be used, so must the execution plan be developed in a similar manner. Thus utilities required to run the equipment need to be commissioned and/or qualified first. Some utilities do require an IQ and/or OQ. For example, a nitrogen system used to overlay a reaction needs to be qualified and in place before it can be used (dry, particle free, N_2, etc.). This would be followed by the equipment in the order in which it will be used. Thus a blender will generally be qualified prior to the granulator.

Good documentation practices

An aspect that is often overlooked in preparing to execute a protocol is to assure that good documentation practices (GDP) for all documentation is maintained. This also means that all recording devices and protocol(s) must be able to be brought into the area where the protocol is to be executed (e.g., clean rooms).[a] All numbers need to be accurate, significant figures correct, and rounding and truncating conditions maintained. An example where GDPs were not maintained is the following:

> An HVAC report (balance, leakage, etc.) was missing a reviewed by (vendor performed) signature and having inconsistent significant figures reported and missing explanations on corrections. The report had been prepared by the vendor/installer. This report was needed to close out part of the HVAC qualification package. How-

---

[a]https://www.pharmout.net/10-steps-to-consider-before-qualification-protocol-execution/.

ever, missing a "reviewed by" signature and the inconsistency in the significant fig-
ure reports of leakage and the missing explanations invalidated the report. It was
sent back to the vendor; this delayed the closure by several weeks.

Another aspect of GDP is to be sure to maintain all pages of the protocol and all data sheets that need to be attached to the protocol. As stated, all data need to be maintained and securely attached to the protocol so as to maintain full data integrity. If pages are added, then it should be noted on the first page of the documents, and the added page should have a unique number (e.g., 3A) as was noted in Chapter 6 on protocol development. Thus, extra pages being added or pages being removed to the protocol, either due to the inability to execute the protocol as written or for other data reasons require a page notation on the first page of the protocol so that reviewers will know exactly what and why the page numbering is altered. If this is not done, it will lead to a deviation and an investigation. Again, any page added to the protocol must have a unique number (i.e., 31A, or 3-1) and needs to be initialed and dated at the time of addition. Any changes to the information entered on a protocol need to be explained (i.e., ~~6.0~~ kg (6.5) NaCl—initial/date explanation: rechecked amount added and corrected). Careful entry of all data will prevent overwrites or other changes "for clarity."

It is recommended to use a copy of the protocol when going into the field for execution. This saves the original so that additional copies can be made if necessary, despite the document being saved on a computer. Also, it allows for "things" to happen during execution (e.g., water spills, a page being and stepped on). REMEMBER, all original data taken/collected MUST be initialed and dated at the time it was performed[b] and be retained in/with the document. Therefore data entered onto the COPY (and marked as a COPY) and used for execution are original data and must be maintained. If a calculation or note is made on a separate piece of paper (not a good idea) during execution, it needs to be firmly attached to the protocol page to which it pertains. Affixing the attachment by paper clip is not sufficient.

Another important aspect of GDP in protocol execution is the page that has all signatures and initials. This page can be separate or attached as part of the protocol. It is easier if it is part of the protocol since reviewers will find the participants much faster. This allows the identification of all those participating in the execution process. Remember protocols have multiple areas for initial and date (in particular IQs) and signatures. These people need to be

---

[b]21 CFR 211.100 (b).

identified in case of questions or investigations that may occur at a later time. In addition, each page or section needs to have a "Performed by" and a "Reviewed by" usually at the bottom of the page. All persons performing any part of the execution on that page need to sign the "Performed by," and a person or equal status or greater (e.g., a manager) can sign the "Reviewed by," or this person from QA will do this at their review. The comment box at the end of the section also should wait to be filled in by QA if there are no comments since they may want to add a comment upon their review.

One last point in filling out the protocol documentation is to never enter data or to write any information necessary for the protocol on the back of any page. Protocols and the data collected need to be only on the front side so that any copies or storage of the protocol by electronic means will be complete.[c]

Test instruments

In dealing with test instruments, one has to be concerned with both sensitivity and specificity. The sensitivity of the instrument will determine the limit of detection (LOD), while specificity will determine what is actually being tested. It is expected that test instruments to be used in the execution of a protocol should be $10X^d$ more sensitive than the measurement to be made. This assures the accuracy needed in recording the results. Thus, if you are measuring to 1 g, the balance should read to a tenth of a gram (1.0 g); otherwise a reading of 1 or 2 g cannot be assured to correct.

Some tests performed during protocol execution may be nonspecific, such as total organic carbon (TOC) for water. This test is still valid as the results are a number related to TOC, while other tests may require higher specificity such as pH or osmolarity. The person performing the execution should know the LOD and specificity of all instruments to be used.

In addition, the test instruments need to be calibrated both before and after each test. This demonstrates that the test instruments have remained in calibration for the duration of the test, and the results are accurate. In some cases the instruments on the equipment itself will be used; these also need to be in calibration prior to beginning of any OQ testing. Calibration is not

[c]S. Ostrove, CGMP presentation, Center for Professional Innovative Education CfPIE), 2019.

[d]United States Pharmacopeia (USP) 40, <41>.

usually required for any testing in the IQ since the IQ only verifies the existence and specifications of the instrument; however, it still may prove necessary.

Putting it all together

First steps

At the start of any protocol execution, the P&ID from which the protocol was derived needs to be reviewed and "walked." This means that the specialist takes the P&ID and looks for each component, pipe, valve, etc. If anything is missing or incorrectly positioned (e.g., a check valve is reversed), it needs to be marked (usually in red) and a deviation listed. After confirming or correcting the error, the "red lined" and signed P&ID can be taken as "AS BUILT." As part of the walk down procedure, many of the IQ items can be verified and completed in the IQ. Sometimes, this walk down is part of the commissioning program. This all depends upon how the company wants to break out the different functions. Following this walk down of the P&ID, the protocol can be executed.

Table 1 shows a brief outline of needed checks to be performed before starting execution.

While executing a qualification, protocol would appear easy; there are many simple pitfalls that can take place. For example, the wrong version of the protocol is executed, the person conducting the execution didn't

Table 1 Preexecution checklist

1. Assure that all instruments on the unit are calibrated
2. Assure that all test instruments to be used are calibrated and their calibration certificate is available for attachment to the protocol
3. Assure that the protocols have been fully approved before starting execution
4. Are trained operators available to run the equipment?
5. Obtain relevant SOPs (draft form is fine up through the OQ)
6. Review the commissioning for the unit. This may have changed a component specification
7. Obtain the current (correct) version of the protocols that are to be executed and review them prior to starting the execution
8. Assure that the equipment is ready and available for the current protocol execution (e.g., it may have been approved for use in or for another product or situation and not the current requirements)
9. Obtain a COPY of the protocol(s) to be executed and assure that all pages are accounted for

get all of the protocol pages, or the equipment is being used for an already validated process.

As already stated, the first step after obtaining the protocol copy is to review the protocols (both IQ and OQ) prior to going out into the field for execution. This would eliminate the confusion when confronted with the actual machine. It also allows the operator a chance to determine if an IQ and OQ test can be combined.

Fig. 1 shows a simplified diagram of the steps needed to complete the execution of the IQ and OQ protocols. Note that the PQ was not included here since it is usually executed as a separate document (but may also be included if the equipment or situation calls for it).

Second steps

Before starting any protocol execution, be sure that the equipment has been commissioned as necessary and is ready to be tested. That is, you know it will work. Table 2 gives a list of items to do at the start of the execution. Please always keep in mind personnel safety and the safety of the equipment.

Upon review of the protocol to be executed, the specialist will know the correct tools needed, the correct recording instruments (pen, bar code readers, etc.), and calibration status of both the unit to be tested and any test instruments to be used.

Follow a logical pattern of execution of the equipment. This means start at things that need to be documented first and to be tested first. (This is the

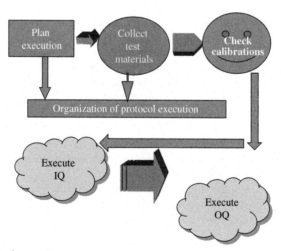

Fig. 1 Outline of execution sequence.

Table 2 Steps in starting a protocol execution

- Review the protocol
  - What is to be tested?
  - Are the tests clear as to how to perform them?
- Collect necessary test instruments
- Review SAFETY procedures
  - LOCKOUT and TAG OUT procedures
  - Specialized equipment
- Notify owners of scheduled validation work
- Notify needed specialists
  - Electricians
  - Plumbers

same order the protocol should have been prepared.) However, that doesn't mean that some tests or verifications can't be skipped for reasons of expediency and returned to at a later time. Recording the data carefully will minimize questions and prevent rejection of the equipment qualification and eventually the process validation. Be sure to follow all GDP practices, number rounding, and truncating rules.

Another important factor in executing a qualification protocol (IQ or OQ) is *"never do anything that will damage or destroy the equipment."* While this sounds like a simplistic idea, it has occurred. For example, pressure relief valves do not have to be tested until they rupture, nor do pumps need to be operated until cavitation to prove the cavitation cut off switch works.

Table 3 provides a list of closing out the execution phase of the protocols. As will be seen in Chapter 11, a final report will need to be prepared, and all deviations will need to be closed prior to considering the executed protocol and the equipment acceptable or useful for their intended purpose.

Third steps
Handling deviations in the protocol
The protocol cannot be considered closed until all deviations from expected values are closed. Remember that the OQ cannot be considered complete until the IQ is complete. Likewise the PQ cannot be considered complete until the OQ is complete. Complete here, in this case, means that all items are successfully executed, and all deviations are investigated and closed. Thus, if an IQ specified a red pump (e.g., for a fire system) and a blue pump was delivered, this is a deviation. Is it acceptable? Probably not acceptable;

Table 3 Completing the execution

---

1. All data/entries to be made on the protocol page
   a. Additional pages may be added if necessary with a unique number
2. All entries should be neat and legible to others
3. No blank lines or spaces
4. Follow GDP requirements
5. The IQ MUST be signed before the OQ can be signed
6. The OQ MUST be signed before the PQ can be signed
7. All deviations (exceptions) MUST be closed prior to signing any protocol as complete (i.e., as built or approved red line drawings need to be available for the IQ [as necessary])
8. All data are entered and either initialed or signed and dated at the time it was executed
9. NO PRE- or POSTDATING IS ALLOWED

---

however, this is a company decision. Another example would be in an OQ; the pump is required to deliver 5 ± 1 GPM, and it delivers 3.5 GPM (not meeting expectations); it would be up to the operation group to make the determination if the pump can be used for its intended purpose (again probably not without some "fix up").

In both cases a determination as to the criticality, the intended use, and the actual delivered unit need to be carefully considered. In addressing protocol deviations, both risk to the operation (e.g., making the product successfully) and risk to the patient need to be considered.

Protocol deviation investigations are not usually handled the same way as manufacturing deviations. As earlier, the risk factors need to be considered, as well as engineering and process design factors. Thus getting a review by the process engineers may be sufficient here.

While investigations as to the reason or correction for a qualification deviation may not be as extensive as one that would be performed for a process failure during production, one certainly needs to be diligent in determining the cause of the event. Most deviations that occur during protocol execution can be easily resolved and corrected. For example,

> During the OQ execution of a water skid system, it was noted that the output flow from water skid was lower than expected. Also the water quality was also not quality the results expected in the protocol. It turned out that the water input and the water output lines were reversed. This caused the still to run with inadequate pressure and lower flow rate, and produce less then acceptable water. The investigation took 3 days to discover the problem. Corrective action—reverse the piping to the correct ports; No preventive action needed.

LESSONS TO BE LEARNED:

(1) Do not make assumptions.

(2) Be sure that all piping is clearly identified and tagged.

(3) Be sure that utility connections are correct and tagged.

(4) Obtain necessary tools to inspect all connections (e.g., mirrors).

(5) Follow manufacture's specifications for installation (i.e., distance from walls, floor, and ceiling).

Thus (1) be sure each of the protocols (IQ then OQ then PQ) is correctly executed in the correct order and (2) do not take shortcuts when installing or moving equipment. The purpose of the protocol is to assure the users that all utilities, all parts, and all functions as necessary for the correct operation (that is the operation needed for the specified function) are correctly and effectively tested, even if it seems irrelevant as in the second case.

Points to remember

1. All personnel who participate in completing any of the testing need to sign the "Executed by" or the "Performed by" (depending on corporate standards) line in the protocol at the time it is performed. This is especially true for portions of the IQ.

2. Be sure to check all equipment when it is moved. A partial requalification will always be needed to be performed to assure that no parts were lost or loosened in the move and that all utility connections are appropriate (e.g., electric polarity)

3. Use commissioning data wherever possible—QA needs to approve.

Summary of protocol execution

1. Prioritize the execution schedule.

2. Review the correct protocol(s) version.

3. Collect all necessary protocol execution tools.

4. Notify the users (as necessary).

5. Assure calibration of all test instruments.

6. Obtain assistance (if necessary).

7. Begin execution.

8. Investigate and close all deviations.

CHAPTER ELEVEN

Protocol reports

Why do you need a qualification report[a]? Should it be a part of the protocol or a prepared as a separate document? These are just two of the questions I've been asked about the preparation of a report closing out the execution of the qualification protocol(s). Preparing a qualification report is an important part of the qualification process as the preparation and execution of the protocols themselves. It is usually recommended to keep it separate from the protocol (s) so that it stands alone and can be reviewed and read independently from the protocol and be able to be handed to a regulatory representative with the idea that it will answer all questions regarding the qualification of the particular unit. However, the regulatory agency may still ask to see the protocol. Again the format of the report is not as important as the content, but it must be complete (especially discussion of the deviations). The report should be a well thought-out summary and scientifically sound and based on the results of the testing obtained from the protocols. It should include all tests and test results performed and a summary of the results in tabular form so that it is easier for the reviewer to understand the data. This is especially important when a large set of numbers are presented (e.g., when temperature mapping studies are reported).

Preparing the report[b]

Usually the lead person on the execution, or protocol, will prepare the report with input from all involved in the qualification process. It should be completed as soon as possible after the completion of the execution of the protocol so that all events that occurred during execution are easily remembered (and addressed if necessary). Actually, all events, deviations, etc. should have been recorded in the protocol, but "why" they occurred is often not included in the notes.

---

[a]Guidelines on validation—Appendix 6 Validation on Qualification of Systems, Utilities, and Equipment, WHO, Draft 2016.
[b]S. Ostrove, "How to Validate a Pharmaceutical Process" Chapter 8, Academic Press, 2016.

Equipment Qualification in the Pharmaceutical Industry
https://doi.org/10.1016/B978-0-12-817568-2.00011-7

In preparing the qualification report, one must keep in mind that the report's function is to summarize all of the qualification work performed. Thus any failures in the required specifications need to be recorded in a deviation log and included with the report. All deviations, whether eventually deemed to be acceptable or not, need to be investigated and reconciled. To prepare a good qualification report, it is necessary to collect the data, analyze the data, and present the data in an easy-to-read format. There should be a header and footer similar to that of the protocol that lists at least the document number (related to the protocol number for easy location). For example, the report number can be R12345, for IQ12345. In addition, the report number should be unique as are the protocol numbers, but it needs to relate to the protocol for reference purposes. It should have the protocol name (equipment with ID), version number (report), and the name of the report.

Table 1 gives a sample of a general table of contents for a qualification report.

As with the preparation of the protocol(s), the IQ and the OQ reports can be and often are combined so as to minimize questions about the results of the testing as shown in Table 2.

When dealing with the PQ, this report is often a separate document.

The final qualification report should start with the conclusion stating that the unit has passed all the IQ and OQ testing specified (assuming it did pass, if not see deviations later). A statement of purpose is followed by a list of all tests with a summary of results (if there is more than one test performed). The report then needs a discussion section for the results so that the impact and reasoning for the specific test can be understood. The discussion section is a very important section of the report since it will demonstrate a full understanding of the logic for the testing and the ability of the team to address the deviation or problem and to provide a logical, scientific, risk-based approach at its justification. If there were any deviations, a list of

Table 1 Sample table of contents IQ/OQ report

- Title
- Approval page
- Conclusion
- Purpose
- Scope
- Tests performed
- Study results
- Deviations log
- Exceptions discussion

Table 2 Sample of a combined IOQ report page

		As specified	As found	Comments
IQ				
Page 4	Capacity	50 gal	55 gal	Question
Page 5	MOC	316 SS	316 SS	Pass
OQ				
Page 15	Flow	5 ± 1 L/min	4.5 L/min	Pass
Page 20	Agitator speed	0–100 RPM	Set = 25 = 25	Pass at all speeds
			Set = 50 = 50	tested
			Set = 95 = 95	

the deviations also needs to be included in the report (addressing deviation investigations is discussed later).

Each section

Approval page

The report needs to have an approval page. This is usually the first page of the report. The approvals need to be from the same departments/groups that approved the protocols. In some select cases, if QA is in agreement or it is company policy, the review and approval of the report are counted as the postapproval of all of the data collected during execution. This is not the usual approach. (Remember in Chapter 6, it was stated that a protocol needs to have a preapproval page and a postapproval page.)

Purpose/scope

Conclusions

As stated earlier, a valid conclusion, as determined by the results of ALL of the testing, needs to be presented at the beginning of the report, not just the tests that passed. In this way a reviewer will know that the unit has been found to be acceptable and that the tests listed were completed. Even if there were deviations from the expectations presented in the protocol(s) and these deviations have been addressed and corrected, the conclusion can report a successful qualification. The team should be proud of successfully completing the qualification—put this up front. The conclusion often starts:

> *The XXXXXX unit has been shown to have all necessary components and has passed all operational testing and is deemed ready for use as intended. A list of all the tests and the results can be found in the results section.*

From this point on a simple summary of the results are presented.

Results

The purpose and scope explain why the protocol was written and why the report was prepared. It also explains what was covered, equipment, site, or system. Presenting the test results along with the expected results as shown in Table 2 for each test in the IQ and OQ and showing or claiming that it passed makes it easier for a reviewer to approve the report and a regulatory review to accept the results without question.

Discussion

The next part of the report is a discussion of the testing based on the results presented and its impact on the product. The discussion should include a reason as to why and how each test was performed. Here, clarity is important so as to allow the reader to refer to the data (results section) as necessary. The discussion should be for each test.

Deviations log

As discussed in Chapter 10, deviations do occur during execution. The report should first present a deviation log of all the deviations encountered during the execution of the protocol. Each deviation should be numbered so as to make reference easy and to easily close out the deviations when complete.

The report should then discuss each of the deviations and provide an explanation as to its cause and present a clear explanation of how it was resolved. Just saying that the deviation does not affect the product is not usually acceptable. The appropriate departments (operation, engineering, etc.) need to have input into determining the cause and to be able to provide a resolution to the event. Prior to finalizing the qualification report, the deviations need to be closed.

If reason for the deviation is not fully resolved, that is, the reason or the root cause was not established and no reason was able to be established, a more intense investigation may be required. However, if a corrective action is found to be required (e.g., the SOP may need to be revised[c]), the report may still be closed as long as the corrective action (e.g., the flow rate is adjusted in the SOP) has been implemented. The following are some considerations that can be used in determining the extent of the investigation report detail:

[c]This is why IQ and OQ protocol executions should be run with DRAFT SOPs.

- How critical is the unit/equipment to the final result of the product?
  - Is the tank painted or not?—Not critical
  - Is the tank heated?—Critical
- Product contact
  - Direct
  - Indirect
  - None
- Is there a preventive action needed to assure the correct operation of the unit (e.g., the SOP needs to be revised)?
- Can the corrective action totally fix the problem (e.g., increasing vacuum time to eliminate air pockets in an autoclave)?

In summary the qualification report needs to be a clear representation of the testing performed, the results obtained, and how they compare with the expected operation or function. Completing the qualification report completes the qualification program, and the equipment can be used as intended.

Definitions and abbreviations

The following is a general list of commonly used terms and abbreviations used in equipment qualification and process validation:

A

Absorptive The ability of a material to get into that material (e.g., a sponge).

Acceptance criteria A set of measurable qualities or specifications used to check out system or equipment installation, operation, or performance. Conformance with these qualities or specifications provides a high degree of confidence that a system is installed, operates, or performs as intended.

Accuracy Expresses the closeness of agreement between the value that is accepted as either a conventional true value or an accepted reference value and the value found.

Air lock Two airtight doors with space in between them.

Alarm Device or function that signals the existence of an abnormal condition by means of an audible or visual change or both.

ANSI American National Standards Institute.

Approval (approved) A document has been approved after it has been reviewed and signed by a group of individuals representing the QA/QC, manufacturing, and engineering disciplines. Other disciplines may partake in the reviews as required.

API Active pharmaceutical ingredient.

ASTM American Society for Testing and Materials.

Audit or quality audit A documented activity performed on a periodic basis in accordance with written procedures to verify, by examination and evaluation of the objective evidence, compliance with those elements of the quality program under review.

B

Bid review The process of reviewing all vendor bids both before they are submitted to the vendor and upon their return. This assures all GMP or URS conditions will be met.

Black box testing Computer systems testing that is only functional tasting.

C

Calibration Comparison of a measurement standard or instrument of known accuracy with another standard or instrument to detect, correlate, report, and/or eliminate any variation in the accuracy of the item being compared.

CDER Center for Drug Evaluation and Research.

Certification Documented testimony by qualified personnel that a system qualification, validation, or revalidation has been performed appropriately and that the results are acceptable.

CFR Code of Federal Regulations.

CGMP (GMP) Current Good Manufacturing Practice.

Change control A formalized program by which qualified representatives review proposed and actual changes to products, processes, equipment, or software to determine their potential impact on the validation status. It provides an audit trail of changes made.

Characteristic A physical, chemical, and functional identifiable property of the product, component, or raw material.

Clean-in-place (CIP) A system of pumps, tanks, and distribution piping designed to circulate detergents, disinfectants, and flushing liquids through process equipment systems without disassembling, hand cleaning, and reassembling the system. CIP systems can be semiautomatically or fully automatically controlled.

Compendial test methods Test methods that appear in official compendiums such as the US Pharmacopeia (USP).

Compliance The state of having all processes under GMP. This includes all relevant equipment qualifications.

Commissioning An engineering function to get the equipment ready for qualification.

Component Any material, substance, part, or assembly used during product manufacture that is intended to be included in the finished product.

Concurrent validation The validation process whereby the equipment or process is tested and qualified during actual production or regular use.

Control testing Testing that verifies switches, controls, and soft keys located on the control panel or associated with FCS operate as designed and in conjunction with equipment and operating parameters.

Control parameter Those operating variables that are utilized to specify conditions under which the product is to be manufactured.

Critical instrumentation Any instrument that provides a record of the process that is used in determining quality of the product.

Critical process parameter (CPP) A process parameter that must be met to meet the expectations of the process so that the product meets its intended criteria (CQA). A change in a CPP results in a change in a CQA.

Critical quality attribute (CQA) A measurable condition that must be met to assure product integrity in structure and/or function. It may be an intermediate stage in the product production and be required to reach the next step or stage.

Critical system (component) A system whose performance has a direct and measurable impact on the quality of the product. A system determined to be a critical system must be designated as such and operated and maintained per approved procedures.

D

Data integrity Assuring that all data and information that are recorded either on paper or by computer are maintained and accurate in all transmissions.

Dead leg A section of piping that does not have full liquid flow. An area that would allow bioburden or product to collect.

Design review A planned, scheduled, and documented audit of pertinent design aspects that can affect performance, safety, or effectiveness.

Detection limit (LOD) Limit of detection. The lowest amount of analyte in a sample that can be detected but not necessarily quantitated as an exact value.

Deviation A result of a protocol test or acceptance criteria that is not in agreement with the expected results expressed in the protocol.

E

Environment The condition, circumstances, influences, and stresses surrounding and affecting the product during storage, handling, transportation, installation, and use.

Equipment qualification (EQ) A combination of IQ, OQ, and possibly PQ protocols into one document for a given piece of equipment.

Excipients Materials used in the process that are not the active ingredient.

F

FAT Factory Acceptance Testing

FDA Food and Drug Administration

Functional Requirement Specifications (FRS) Requirements used by the engineering group in the design of the conditions specified in the URS.

Functional testing Testing that includes manual and automatic testing verifying components within the system (valves, etc.) and the system as a whole operates as designed and in conjunction with equipment and operating parameters.

G

Gray box testing Computer system testing that combines functional and structural testing but is primarily functional testing.

H

Hardware The physical components of an electronic control system (as contrasted with the software components). These components provide the physical connections to the system(s) or equipment to be controlled. Hardware components include (but are not limited to) the central processing unit (CPU—microprocessor), input/output (I/O—sensors and printers), and relays.

HEPA filters High-efficiency particulate air filters.

HPLC High-performance liquid chromatography or high-pressure liquid chromatography.

HVAC Heating, ventilation, and air conditioning.

I

ICH International Council on Harmonization.

Installation qualification (IQ) Documented verification that key aspects of the installation adhere to appropriate codes, approved design specifications, and manufacturer's recommendations (where appropriate).

Investigation The process of determining the reason for an error or noncompliance to a protocol specification.

L

LIMS Laboratory information management system.

Laboratory qualification The process by which the staff, instrumentation, and all relevant support systems in a laboratory are demonstrated to be capable of carrying out a test method and consistently generate correct results in accordance with predetermined acceptance criteria.

Ladder logic A diagrammatically representation of the specific functions of an electronic control system for PLCs.

Linearity Is the assay's ability (within a given range) to obtain test results that are directly proportional to the concentration (amount) of analyte in the sample.

M

Material of construction (MOC) The major material that the unit is made up from. It pertains to product contact areas primarily.

Method development The process by which new methods are developed and evaluated for suitability of use as test methods.

Method transfer The process by which methods are transferred from the transferring laboratory to receiving laboratories such that performance characteristics are retained within defined acceptance criteria. The transfer process should include qualification of the laboratory to use the method.

Method validation The process by which attributes such as accuracy, precision, selectivity, ruggedness, and reproducibility of developed methods are formally established against predefined acceptance criteria and documented. Except for stability indication, compendial methods may only require abbreviated method validation studies (e.g., accuracy, linearity, and bias).

N

NIST National Institute of Standards and Technology.

Noncritical instrumentation Instrumentation used primarily for convenience, operator ease, or maintenance.

O

Operating parameter or variable Those process variables that are measured to monitor the state of the process.

Operational qualification (OQ) Documented verification that systems or subsystems, capable of being changed, perform as intended throughout anticipated operating ranges.

OSHA Occupational Safety and Health Administration.

P

PAR Proved acceptable range.

Passivation Removing and smoothing the surface of stainless steel units so as to make them less reactive.

P&ID Piping and instrumentation drawing (schematic representation of the installed piping and instruments).

Performance qualification (PQ) Documented verification that equipment, systems, or processes perform as intended throughout specified operating ranges.

PFD Process flow drawing (diagram).

pH Logarithmic measurement of the acidity or alkalinity of a solution.

PLC Programmed logic controller.

Precision Expresses the closeness of agreement (degree of scatter) between a series of measurements obtained from sampling of the same homogenous sample under the prescribed conditions. Precision may be considered at three levels: repeatability, intermediate precision, and reproducibility.

Protocol Written testing plan that includes the objectives and methods for the conduct of a study.

PPQ Process performance qualification.

Process validation (now process performance qualification, PPQ) Obtaining documented evidence that the process or production of the pharmaceutical product meets the preapproved acceptance criteria for that product.

Prospective validation (or qualification) A defined strategy of test procedures that in combination with routine production methods and quality control techniques provides documented assurance that a system is performing as intended and/or that a product conforms to its predetermined specifications.

Preventative maintenance The program or procedures used to keep all process systems fully operating within accepted predefined specifications.

Proved acceptable range (PAR) Those values of a control or operating parameter that fall between the proved upper and lower operating conditions (validated ranges). The PAR values are derived from developmental validation studies whose intent is, primarily, to establish the operational ranges to be used in the production environment.

Q

Qualification The procedure by which equipment, processes, and instrumentation are proved to be designed properly and perform adequately and reproducibility as designed.

Quality The composite of the characteristics, including performance, of an item or product.

Quality assurance (QA) program requirements As defined in the GMP, the requirements consist of procedures adequate to assure the quality of the manufacturing process and adequate to assure that the following functions are performed: (1) review of production records; (2) approval or rejection of components, drug product containers, closures, in-process materials, packaging materials, labeling, and drug products and approval or rejection of drug products manufactured, processed, packaged, or held under contract by another company; (3) availability of adequate laboratory facilities for testing and, based on test results, determining disposition of components, drug product containers, closures, packaging materials, in-process materials, and drug products; and (4) approval or rejection of procedures and specifications impacting on the strength, quality, and purity of the drug product.

Quality control (QC) unit A regulatory process whereby the quality of raw materials and produced product is controlled by inspection and tested for the purpose of preventing production of defective product. This unit is composed of QA and QC.

Qualification of methods The process by which methods are determined to be suitable for the analysis of a given test article by a given laboratory.

Quantitation limit Is the lowest amount of analyte in a sample that can be quantitatively determined with suitable precision and accuracy.

Quarantine Any area that is marked, designated, or set aside for the holding of incoming components prior to acceptance examination and finished products until released.

R

Range Is the interval between the upper and lower concentration (amounts) of analyte in the sample (including these concentrations) for which it has been demonstrated that the analytic procedure has a suitable level of precision, accuracy, and linearity.

Reference instrumentation Any instrument excluded from the calibration program because of its inability to be calibrated or its infrequency of use.

Regulatory test method A test method that has been approved by a governmental regulatory agency such as the FDA.

Repeatability Expresses the precision under the same operating conditions over a short interval of time. Repeatability is also referred to as "intraassay precision."

Reproducibility Expresses the precision between laboratories (collaborative studies, usually applied to standardization of methodology).

Retrospective validation Performing analysis on previous batch records for a given operation. A sufficient number of batches or production runs must be used in the analysis to demonstrate reproducibility and compliance with CGMP regulations overall.

Rework A set of procedures that define the conditions under which a process or batch of product can be mixed into or otherwise redone so as to make it conform to the required specifications for that product.

Risk management Determining the risk that an operation or a unit will have on the final product and/or the patient.

Robustness Is a measure of the assay's capacity to remain unaffected by small but deliberate variations in method parameters and provides an indication of its reliability during normal usage.

R&D Research and development.

Revalidation The repetition of the validation process or a specific portion of it, to assure that a system is suitable for use after modification or repair. Revalidation is required on a periodic basis to ensure that the process or system continues to operate as intended.

S

Site Acceptance Test (SAT) Testing and verifying the equipment is intact upon receipt at the facility and ready for commissioning.

Software The portion of an electronic control system composed of instructions written in one or more artificial language(s). Some are readable as standard English and others, for example, binary, that are only readable by machine or those extremely well versed in the "machine language." These instructions provide the specific directions to the electronic control system to perform various functions. Software is frequently user (or self) alterable. This alterability of software results in greater flexibility of the system and greater risk. This risk is offset by instigating software change control measures and security access and using compiled code.

Source code The code used by computers or controllers of process systems or equipment. This code is readable only by the machine components themselves (frequently this code is binary) and can be very specific to the particular machine components in question. Most humans cannot write software directly in machine-readable (compiled) code; therefore humans typically write code in a higher-order language such as COBOL and FORTRAN. This human-readable code is called the source code (because it is the source of the machine-readable code). This source code is compiled (translated) by a computer system from the human-readable form to the machine-readable form.

Startup/commissioning (S/C) The program or procedure used to perform preliminary testing on equipment or utilities. It provides documentation that the equipment is connected according to design specifications and that the basic operation is achievable.

Standard operating procedure (SOP) Written instructions that enable a trained person to operate or otherwise perform a given function.

Sanitization Reduction in the number of microorganisms to a safe or relatively safe level as determined by applicable regulations or the purpose of application.

Sanitizer Any chemical that kills microbial contamination in the form of vegetative cells.

Sensitivity The lowest measurement that can be made for a particular test.

Specificity Is the ability to assess unequivocally the analyte in the presence of components that may be expected to be present.

Set point The setting made on a piece of equipment that the unit is supposed to run.

State of control A condition in which operating and control parameters of processes or systems are stable and within ranges documented to establish consistent and reliable control of the processes.

Stand-alone system A single unit of process equipment or a group of process equipment that will function as a single unit.

Structural testing Those tests on computer systems that include hardware and software testing. This includes, but not limited to, software version and source code development.

System A number of integrated steps, functions, and items of equipment that must be considered as a unit to assure supply of a consistent, uniform, and high-quality component for the manufacture of a product.

System boundary The upper and lower limits that a unit can operate at.

System suitability Specific tests designed to determine the suitability of the overall test system (including instrumentation, sample preparation, and analyst) is suitable for the intended use of the test method. Typical tests utilized for system suitability measure test system precision, specificity, and detection.

T

Transfer area Any area of the manufacturing facility, other than the weighing, mixing, or filling areas, where the components, in-process materials, and drug products, and drug product contact surfaces of equipment, containers, and closures after final rinse of such surfaces, are exposed to the plant environment.

Testing Qualified activities performed by the testing laboratory, utilizing approved, validated, qualified, and (if appropriate) successfully transferred methods. These activities accomplish the purpose of establishing testing procedures to ensure accurate determination of the identity, strength, quality, and purity of the component/product tested.

Testing laboratory The laboratory that performs routine testing for official disposition (e.g., release and stability) of components and/or products. The testing laboratory may be a QA laboratory at a manufacturing site or a contract laboratory whose use is approved in accord with corporate policies/procedures.

Test method An approved detailed procedure describing how to test a sample for a specified attribute (e.g., assay), the amount required, instrumentation, reagents, sample preparation steps, data generation steps, and calculations used for evaluation.

Test results The final calculated results obtained after testing has been completed.

U

USP US Pharmacopeia.

User Requirement Specifications (URS) Those requirements required by the user for the operation of the equipment for the process.

V

Validation The process of demonstrating or proving that the process will function as expected.

Validation Master Plan (VMP) A plan prepared for a project or site that summarizes all items to be qualified and validated.

Validation protocol An approved document stating how validation is conducted. The document includes test parameters, product characteristics, required equipment, and procedures and acceptance criteria.

Validation Final Report An approved document of the results derived from executing a validation protocol. The report includes a brief summary of conclusions based on test results of the validation status. Proved acceptable ranges for critical process parameters are designated as determined by the results of the validation study.

Verify (verification) Comparison of a measurement standard of known accuracy with another standard or instrument to detect, correlate, or report, but not eliminate, any variation in the accuracy of the item being compared. Verification implies that no adjustment of the compared item is possible with reestablish accuracy.

W

White-box testing Computer system qualification that includes full functional and structural testing.

Worst case A set of conditions encompassing upper and lower processing limits and circumstances, including those within standard operating procedures, which pose the greatest chance of process or product failure when compared with ideal conditions. Such conditions do not necessarily induce product or process failure.

PREPARING A QUALIFICATION PROTOCOL

Purpose:

This procedure will describe the steps to be taken for the preparation of validation protocols. This applies to the Installation Qualification (IQ), the Operational Qualification (OQ) and the Performance Qualification (PQ).

Scope:

This procedure applies to all Qualification protocols prepared by OAI. This procedure may be modified if required by the client upon approval of the project manager and the head of the Validation Department.

Procedure:

1. Collect relevant documentation – reference Equipment History File
    a. Manuals
        i. Operation
        ii. Cleaning
        iii. Preventive Maintenance
    b. Drawings
        i. Engineering
        ii. Vendor
    c. Specs
        i. User
        ii. Functional
    d. SOPs (as required by the system/equipment)
    e. Purchase Orders
    f. Others as needed
2. Search Validation Library for analogous equipment /system
    a. Obtain equipment Check list
3. Obtain correct protocol format from client/office file
4. Protocols will be prepared using TIMES NEW ROMAN font in 12 pt type unless otherwise specified by the client.
    a. Covers for the protocols will be in TIMES NEW ROMAN font 18-24 pt in **BOLD** type face.
5. Prepare IQ Draft
    a. Author Reviews and Edits
    b. OAI Validation Management Review
6. If acceptable, the protocol is saved on an External floppy disk or equivalent device.
7. Submitted to client for review
8. If acceptable the protocol is routed for signature
9. Author starts preparation of OQ Draft upon submission to OAI validation management

PREPARING A QUALIFICATION PROTOCOL

10. Repeat steps 2-7 for OQ
11. Repeat steps 2-7 for PQ if required
12. Protocol format
    a. Header
        i. Revision Number
        ii. Protocol Title
        iii. Company Name
        iv. Date of preparation
    b. Footer
        i. Page X of Y (THIS CAN BE N THE HEADER)
13. Signatures
    a. Each section needs to have a COMPLETED BY and a REVIEWED BY signature verifying completion of each section
    b. The protocol needs to have been PRE-APPROVED prior to execution
    c. The same persons pre-approving the protocol need to approve the protocol upon completion
14. Protocol Contents
    a. Pre-Approval
    b. Purpose
    c. Scope
    d. Definitions
    e. Responsibilities
    f. Tests
    g. References
    h. Summary
    i. Post-Approval
15. Flow sheet of protocol development can be seen in Attachment A

Attachment A
    Flow Diagram(s)

IQ – OQ – PQ Utility

The protocol(s) shown in this section are real and have been adapted and modified for this use. I have also removed duplicate tests or pages, e.g., two UV lights, filters, or other multiple units – as the flow diagram would indicate. I have tried to keep the numbering correct but errors may have occurred due to pagination changes.

Stand Alone Equipment

The second protocol – Shelf Dryer – is an example of a combination protocol (IQ, OQ, PQ). Note the style is similar but not quite the same as the individual IQ, OQ, and PQ. As stated, it is the content that is important.

Installation Qualification Protocol
for the
USP Water System

PREPARED FOR:

Company
City, State

PREPARED BY:
(NOTE: IF PREPARED BY AN OUTSIDE COMPANY)

Xxxxxx
City, State

Protocol No.:
Revision No.: 0
Date:

	USP WATER SYSTEM INSTALLATION QUALIFICATION PROTOCOL		Page 2 of 24
Protocol No.:	Effective Date:	Revision No.: 0	Supersedes: None

TABLE OF CONTENTS

	USP WATER SYSTEM INSTALLATION QUALIFICATION PROTOCOL		Page 3 of 24
Protocol No.:	Effective Date:	Revision No.: 0	Supersedes: None

Revision Record

Revision	Date	Changes
A		Draft
0		Original

	USP WATER SYSTEM INSTALLATION QUALIFICATION PROTOCOL		Page 4 of 24
Protocol No.:	Effective Date:	Revision No.: 0	Supersedes: None

USP Water System
Installation Qualification Protocol
Protocol Number:

PROTOCOL PREPARED BY: _____ _____ DAT E: _____
                                                    Xxxxxx

PROTOCOL APPROVED BY

VALIDATION: _____ _____ D ATE: _____ __
                                      COMPANY

ENGINEERING: _____
                                                              DATE:
                                       COMPANY

OPERATIONS: _____ DATE: _____   _
                                      COMPANY

QUALITY ASSURANCE: _____   DATE:
                                     COMPANY

PROTOCOL APPROVAL SIGNIFIES CONCURRENCE WITH THE TESTS, PROCEDURES AND
ACCEPTANCE CRITERIA OUTLINED HEREIN.

	USP WATER SYSTEM INSTALLATION QUALIFICATION PROTOCOL		Page 5 of 24
Protocol No.:	Effective Date:	Revision No.: 0	Supersedes: None

1.0   PURPOSE

This protocol describes the Installation Qualification requirements and corresponding acceptance criteria for Company's USP Water (USP) System located in City, State. The installation and testing of this system will be consistent with the company's Change Control program (SOP XXXXXX) and current Good Manufacturing Practices. This Installation Qualification (IQ) verifies that all major components of the system meet or exceed design requirements established by Company.

2.0   SYSTEM/EQUIPMENT DESCRIPTION

2.1   GENERAL

The USP Water System (USP) system will provide U.S.P. Water for use in any operations requiring U.S.P. Water at the Company-Facility.

2.2   DESIGN REQUIREMENTS AND EQUIPMENT RATIONAL

The USP Water System must be capable of supplying USP grade water at the required capacity, pressure and quality.

2.3   System Block Diagram

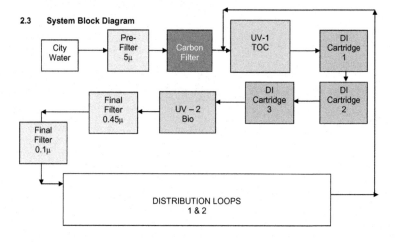

	USP WATER SYSTEM INSTALLATION QUALIFICATION PROTOCOL		Page 6 of 24
Protocol No.:	Effective Date:	Revision No.: 0	Supersedes: None

3.0 DOCUMENTATION

The section will detail the documentation required to verify that the installation of the USP Water System adheres to the manufacturer's and Company's requirements and approved design specifications.

3.1 ENGINEERING DOCUMENTATION

3.1.1 List all of the engineering documentation that pertains to the design, purchase and installation of the USP Water System. The documentation to be listed may include, but not be limited to the following list.

- As Built Drawings
- P&ID's
- Design Specifications
- Purchase Orders
- Manuals (Operation, Maintenance, Cleaning)
- Vendor test results and certificates
- Materials of Construction and certificates (as appropriate)
- Weld reports
- Start-up Reports (commissioning)
- Spare Parts list
- PLC documentation (as appropriate)

  PLC Documentation may include, but is not limited to: System architecture overview, standards and terminology listing, hardware design overview, assembly details, interface hardware design, trip and interlock design, I/O maps and point database, and security system documentation

3.1.2 Record document title, number, revision/date and location. (if applicable) in the following table

3.1.3 Acceptance Criteria:
- All drawings / documents must accurately represent the water system as installed.
- All documents must be current and the latest version listed

	USP WATER SYSTEM INSTALLATION QUALIFICATION PROTOCOL		Page 7 of 24	
Protocol No.:	Effective Date:	Revision No.: 0	Supersedes: None	

3.1 ENGINEERING DOCUMENTATION (Cont.)

TITLE	DOCUMENT NUMBER	ISSUE DATE	REV #.	LOCATION
SOP				
Servicing the USP Water System			1	QA
USP Purified Water Monitoring Program			3	QA
Sanitization of the Purified Water Distribution System			0	QA
Dispensing USP Purified Water from the USP Water Distribution System			0	QA
DRAWINGS				
USP Water Distribution System			3	QA
USP Water System			3	QA

COMMENTS: _____ _____

_____ _____

_____ _____

4.0 ALARMS
Alarms List

Conducted By: _____ Date: _____ _____

Reviewed By: _____ Date: _____ _____

	USP WATER SYSTEM INSTALLATION QUALIFICATION PROTOCOL		Page 8 of 24
Protocol No.:	Effective Date:	Revision No.: 0	Supersedes: None

Alarm	Type	Location	Set Point	Date/By
TOC	Audible	On TOC meter	xxxxppb	

COMMENTS:

_____   _____
_____   _____
_____   _____
_____   _____
_____   _____

Conducted By: _____ Date: _____   _____

Reviewed By: _____ Date: _____   _____

	USP WATER SYSTEM INSTALLATION QUALIFICATION PROTOCOL		Page 9 of 24
Protocol No.:	Effective Date:	Revision No.: 0	Supersedes: None

5.0 Major Components

5.1 Complete the following tables that define each of the major components of the USP Water System. Document the following where applicable:

- Component Name
- Description / Function
- Manufacturer
- Model/Part Number
- Serial Number
- Company Asses Number
- Location
- Component Specific Information
- Materials of Construction (MOC)

List of major components

- Carbon Filter
- Pre, Intermediate and Final Filter
- Mixed Bed Canisters
- Pressurization/Circulation Pump
- Ultraviolet Disinfector(s)
- Heat Exchanger
- USP Distribution Pump
- USP Distribution Loop
- USP Distribution Loop Heat Exchanger

5.2 Verify that each component is installed and identified as shown on the respective P&ID(s), and that each component conforms to design and/or purchase specifications.

5.3 Acceptance Criteria:

- Each component must be identified as specified.
- Each component must meet the design and/or purchase specifications.
- Must meet COMPANY specifications.
- A response of "Yes" is required for items which require a Yes / No response.
- Any response of "No" must be explained in the comment section.

	USP WATER SYSTEM INSTALLATION QUALIFICATION PROTOCOL		Page 10 of 24
Protocol No.:	Effective Date:	Revision No.: 0	Supersedes: None

5.0   MAJOR COMPONENT LIST (Cont.)

Component: Carbon Filter

Description: Removes Organics and Chlorine from the City Water.

	AS SPECIFIED	AS FOUND	By/Date
COMPANY ASSET NUMBER			
MANUFACTURER			
MODEL NUMBER			
SERIAL NUMBER			
CAPACITY			
Vessel MOC			
DIMENSIONS	"		

	YES / NO
Component meets design and/or purchase specifications.	
Component is mounted and secured according to specifications.	

COMMENTS: _____   _____

_____   _____

_____   _____

_____   _____

_____   _____

_____   _____

Conducted By: _____ Date: _____   _____

Reviewed By: _____ Date: _____   _____

	USP WATER SYSTEM INSTALLATION QUALIFICATION PROTOCOL		Page 11 of 24
Protocol No.:	Effective Date:	Revision No.: 0	Supersedes: None

5.0   MAJOR COMPONENT LIST (Cont.)

Component: PUMP - Centrifugal

Description: Pressurization / Recirculation.

PUMP DATA	AS SPECIFIED	AS FOUND	By/Date
COMPANY ASSET NUMBER			
MANUFACTURER			
MODEL/PART NUMBER			
SERIAL NUMBER			
MOC			
SEAL TYPE			
CAPACITY			
SIZE			
LUBRICATION			

MOTOR DATA	AS SPECIFIED	AS FOUND	By/Date
MANUFACTURER			
MODEL NUMBER			
SERIAL NUMBER			
HP/Volts/Phase			
HERTZ			
FULL LOAD AMPS			
MOTOR FRAME			
ENCLOSURE			
ROTATION DIRECTION			
RATED RPM			

	YES / NO
Component meets design and/or purchase specifications.	
Component is mounted and secured according to specifications.	

COMMENTS: _____   _____

Conducted By: _____ Date: _____   _____

Reviewed By: _____ Date: _____   _____

	USP WATER SYSTEM INSTALLATION QUALIFICATION PROTOCOL		Page 12 of 24
Protocol No.:	Effective Date:	Revision No.: 0	Supersedes: None

5.0   MAJOR COMPONENT LIST (Cont.)

Component: FILTER

Description: 5u

HOUSING	AS SPECIFIED	AS FOUND	By/Date
COMPANY ASSET NUMBER			
MANUFACTURER			
MODEL NUMBER			
SERIAL NUMBER			
CONFIGURATION/SIZE			
PRESSURE RATING			
MATERIAL OF CONSTRUCTION			

CARTRIDGE	AS SPECIFIED	AS FOUND	By/Date
MANUFACTURER			
MODEL NUMBER			
TYPE (Hydrophobic/Hydrophilic)			
PRESSURE DIFFERENTIAL RATING			
MATERIAL OF CONSTRUCTION			

	YES / NO
Component meets design and/or purchase specifications.	
Component is mounted and secured according to specifications.	

COMMENTS: _____   _____

_____   _____

_____   _____

_____   _____

_____   _____

_____   _____

Conducted By: _____ Date: _____   _____

Reviewed By: _____ Date: _____   _____

	USP WATER SYSTEM INSTALLATION QUALIFICATION PROTOCOL		Page 13 of 24
Protocol No.:	Effective Date:	Revision No.: 0	Supersedes: None

5.0   MAJOR COMPONENT LIST (Cont.)

Component: ULTRAVIOLET LIGHT

Description: 254 nm

	AS SPECIFIED	AS FOUND	BY/DATE
COMPANY ASSET NUMBER			
MANUFACTURER			
MODEL NUMBER			
SERIAL NUMBER			
UV LAMP CONFIGURATION			
MATERIAL OF CONSTRUCTION			
WETTED SURFACES MOC			
CABINET MOC			
SLEEVE MOC			
CAPACITY			
OPTICAL SENSOR MODEL NUMBER			
OVERHEAT PROTECTION			
VOLT/AMP/HZ			

	YES / NO
Component meets design and/or purchase specifications.	
Component is mounted and secured according to specifications.	

COMMENTS: _____   _____

_____   _____

_____   _____

_____   _____

	USP WATER SYSTEM INSTALLATION QUALIFICATION PROTOCOL		Page 14 of 24
Protocol No.:	Effective Date:	Revision No.: 0	Supersedes: None

5.0   MAJOR COMPONENT LIST (Cont.)

Component: MIXED BED EXCHANGE CANISTER

Description: DEIONIZATION

	AS SPECIFIED	AS FOUND	BY/DATE
COMPANY ASSET NUMBER			
MANUFACTURER			
MODEL NUMBER			
SERIAL NUMBER			
CANISTER MOC			
INLET/OUTLET CONNECTION TYPE			
CANISTER DIMENSIONS			
RESIN TYPE			
RESIN AMOUNT			

	YES / NO
Component meets design and/or purchase specifications.	
Component is mounted and secured according to specifications.	

COMMENTS: _____
_____
_____
_____
_____

PIPING VERIFICATION

3.3.1   Review as-built P&IDs. Verify that each section of piping is installed as shown on the respective P&ID(s), and that each section of piping conforms to design and/or purchase specifications. Document any exceptional conditions found in the field.

3.3.2   Acceptance Criteria:
  • Each section of piping must conform to design and/or purchase specifications.
  • Attach or reference location of drawing (as built)

COMMENTS: _____
_____
_____
_____

Conducted By: _____ Date: _____

Reviewed By: _____ Date: _____

	USP WATER SYSTEM INSTALLATION QUALIFICATION PROTOCOL		Page 15 of 24
Protocol No.:	Effective Date:	Revision No.: 0	Supersedes: None

VALVE VERIFICATION

3.4.1   Complete the following table or attach applicable list that defines the valves of the USP Water System. Document the following where applicable:

- Tag Number
- Valve Type
- Manufacturer
- Model Number
- Size
- Materials of Construction (MOC)

3.4.2   Verify that each valve is installed and identified as shown on the respective P&ID(s) and that each valve conforms to design and/or purchase specifications.

3.4.3   Acceptance Criteria:

- Each valve must conform to design and/or purchase specifications.
- A response of "Yes" is required for items which require a Yes / No response.
- Any response of "No" must be explained in the comment section.

	USP WATER SYSTEM INSTALLATION QUALIFICATION PROTOCOL	Page 16 of 24
Protocol No.:	Effective Date: Revision No.: 0	Supersedes: None

VALVE VERIFICATION (Cont.)

COMPANY ASSET NUMBER	Valve Type	Manufacturer	Automatic/ Manual	Size (in)	MOC	Line No.	Location	Default Position (O/C)	Initial / Date

Conducted By: _____ Date: _____

Reviewed By: _____ Date: _____

	USP WATER INSTALLATION QUALIFICATION PROTOCOL		Page 17 of 24
Protocol No.:	Effective Date:	Revision No.: 0	Supersedes: None

INSTRUMENTATION VERIFICATION

5.3.1 Complete the following table or attach appropriate instrument schedule, which defines the instrumentation of the USP Water System. List all instruments that are part of the system and separate into critical and non-critical. Each instrument will be verified as conforming to specifications, proper installation and identification. Document the following where applicable:

- Company Asset Number
- Instrument Name
- Manufacturer
- Model Number
- Serial Number
- Range
- Materials of Construction (MOC) [Required only if instrumentation is in direct contact with product]

5.3.2 Verify that each instrument is installed as shown on the respective P&ID(s) and that each instrument conforms to design and/or purchase specifications.

5.3.4 Acceptance Criteria:

Critical:

- Each instrument must conform to design and/or purchase specifications.
- Each instrument must be part of the Plant Calibration Program.
- Each critical instrument, which comes into contact with product, must be of appropriate materials of construction.

Non-critical:

- Each instrument must conform to design and/or purchase specifications.

Conducted By: _____ Date: _____

Reviewed By: _____ Date: _____

	USP WATER INSTALLATION QUALIFICATION PROTCOL		Page 18 of 24
Protocol No.:	Effective Date:	Revision No.: 0	Supersedes: None

INSTRUMENTATION VERIFICATION (Cont.)

COMPAN Y Asset Number	Description	MOC	Critical / Non-Critical	Mfg. / Model No.	Serial No.	Range	Cal. Date	Calibration Frequency	Initial / Date

COMMENTS: _____

_____

_____

Conducted By: _____ Date: _____

Reviewed By: _____ Date: _____

	USP WATER INSTALLATION QUALIFICATION PROTOCOL		Page 19 of 24
Protocol No.:	Effective Date:	Revision No.: 0	Supersedes: None

INSTRUMENTATION VERIFICATION (Cont.)

Component: PROGRAMMABLE CONTROLLER
Description: _____

	AS SPECIFIED	AS FOUND	BY/DATE
COMPANY ASSET NUMBER			
MANUFACTURER			
MODEL NUMBER			
SERIAL NUMBER (Controller)			
SERIAL NUMBER (Memory)			
SERIAL NUMBER (Exp. Unit)			
NUMBER OF ANALOG INPUTS			
NUMBER OF ANALOG OUTPUTS			
NUMBER OF DIGITAL INPUTS			
NUMBER OF DIGITAL OUTPUTS			
SOURCE CODE # AND REVISION			
SOURCE CODE LOCATION			
SECURITY LEVEL PLAN			

	YES / NO
Component meets design and/or purchase specifications.	
Component is mounted and secured according to specifications.	

COMMENTS: _____ _____

_____ _____
_____ _____
_____ _____
_____ _____

Conducted By: _____ Date: _____ _____

Reviewed By: _____ Date: _____ _____

	USP WATER SYSTEM INSTALLATION QUALIFICATION PROTOCOL		Page 20 of 24
Protocol No	Effective Date:	Revision No.: 0	Supersedes: None

INSTRUMENTATION VERIFICATION (Cont.)

Component: CONTROL PANEL
Description: _____

	AS SPECIFIED	AS FOUND	BY/DATE
COMPANY ASSET NUMBER			
MANUFACTURER			
MODEL NUMBER			
SERIAL NUMBER			

INDICATOR LAMPS	TYPE	PURPOSE	BY/DATE

	USP WATER SYSTEM INSTALLATION QUALIFICATION PROTOCOL		Page 21 of 24
Protocol No	Effective Date:	Revision No.: 0	Supersedes: None

INSTRUMENTATION VERIFICATION (Cont.)

Component: CONTROL PANEL (Cont.)

SWITCHES	TYPE	PURPOSE	BY/DATE

	YES / NO
Component meets design and/or purchase specifications.	
Component is mounted and secured according to specifications.	

COMMENTS: _____   _____

_____   _____

_____   _____

_____   _____

_____   _____

	USP WATER SYSTEM INSTALLATION QUALIFICATION PROTOCOL		Page 22 of 24
Protocol No	Effective Date:	Revision No.: 0	Supersedes: None

6.0   EXCEPTIONAL CONDITIONS

Discrepancies may be observed as the protocol is being executed. Should this occur, an "Exceptional Condition Report" is to be prepared. The exceptional Condition Report" is to identify the discrepancy found, project the impact, and suggest recommendations. In conjunction with COMPANY, a plan of action will be determined and an appropriate corrective action taken.

EXCEPTIONAL CONDITION REPORT

Date: _____   #_____

Discrepancy:

_____   _____
_____   _____
_____   _____
_____   _____
_____   _____

Impact:

_____   _____
_____   _____
_____   _____
_____   _____

Recommendations:

_____   _____
_____   _____
_____   _____
_____   _____

Corrective Action: Due Date: _____

_____   _____
_____   _____
_____   _____
_____   _____

____ Critical Deviation   ____ Non-Critical Deviation

State reason why Deviation is classifies as non-critical: _____

_____   _____

Satisfactorily Completed (Y/N): _____

	USP WATER SYSTEM INSTALLATION QUALIFICATION PROTOCOL		Page 23 of 24
Protocol No	Effective Date:	Revision No.: 0	Supersedes: None

7.0   FINAL REPORT STATEMENT

A final report will be written after the execution of this protocol. This report will be a stand alone document presentable to the regulatory agencies. The contents of the report, along with the protocol, will contain all data relevant to this qualification. The report will also include Exceptional Conditions found along with the applicable resolutions. The report will be reviewed and signed by the pertinent Validation Support Team members and the Validation Manager. The final report and the protocol will be used for certification of the equipment / system.

	USP WATER INSTALLATION QUALIFICATION PROTOCOL		Page 24 of 24
Protocol No.:	Effective Date:	Revision No.: 0	Supersedes: None

8.0   FINAL APPROVAL SIGNATURES

All items in the Installation Qualification of the USP Water System have been reviewed and found to be acceptable. All variations or discrepancies have been satisfactorily resolved. Therefore, this USP Water System is ready for Operational Qualification.

PROTOCOL REVIEWED BY: _____   DA   TE: _____
                                                      Xxxxxx

PROTOCOL APPROVED BY

VALIDATION: _____   DATE: _____
                                                      COMPANY

ENGINEERING: _____   DATE:_____
                                                      COMPANY

OPERATIONS: _____   DATE: ___   ___
                                                      COMPANY

QUALITY ASSURANCE: _____ _____   DATE: _____
                                                      COMPANY

Operational Qualification Protocol
for the
USP Water System

PREPARED FOR:

Company
City, State

PREPARED BY:
XXXXXX
City, State

Protocol No.:
Revision No.: 0
Date:

	USP WATER SYSTEM OPERATIONAL QUALIFICATION PROTOCOL		Page 2 of 27
Protocol No.: Relate to IQ	Effective Date:	Revision No.: 0	Supersedes: None

TABLE OF CONTENTS

	USP WATER SYSTEM OPERATIONAL QUALIFICATION PROTOCOL		Page 3 of 24
Protocol No.: Relate to IQ	Effective Date:	Revision No.: 0	Supersedes: N/A

Revision Record

Revision	Date	Changes
A		Draft
0		Original

	USP WATER SYSTEM OPERATIONAL QUALIFICATION PROTOCOL		Page 4 of 24
Protocol No.: Relate to IQ	Effective Date:	Revision No.: 0	Supersedes: N/A

USP Water System
Operational Qualification Protocol
Protocol Number:

PROTOCOL PREPARED BY: _____ DATE: _____
                                                            Signature
                                               Print _____

PROTOCOL APPROVED BY:

VALIDATION: _____ DATE: _____
                                        COMPANY
                                        Signature
                           Print _____

ENGINEERING: _____ DATE: _____
                                         COMPANY
                                         Signature
                            Print _____

OPERATIONS: _____ DATE: _____
                                        COMPANY
                                        Signature
                           Print _____

QUALITY ASSURANCE _____ DATE: _____
                                              COMPANY
                                              Signature
                                 Print _____

PROTOCOL APPROVAL SIGNIFIES CONCURRENCE WITH THE TESTS, PROCEDURES AND
ACCEPTANCE CRITERIA OUTLINED HEREIN.

	USP WATER SYSTEM OPERATIONAL QUALIFICATION PROTOCOL		Page 5 of 24
Protocol No.: Relate to IQ	Effective Date:	Revision No.: 0	Supersedes: N/A

1.0 GENERAL

This protocol defines the Operational Qualification requirements and the corresponding acceptance criteria for a USP Water System located at the COMPANY, Inc. facilities in City, state.

2.0 SYSTEM/EQUIPMENT DESCRIPTION

2.1 GENERAL

The USP Water System will provide USP grade Purified Water for use in manufacturing processes at Company's facility.

2.2 DESIGN REQUIREMENTS

The USP Water System must be capable of supplying Purified Water at Company's specified capacity, pressure, and quality.

2.3 RECOMMENDED VALIDATION EQUIPMENT

Validation equipment that may be required for the execution of this protocol includes, but is not limited to:

Calibrated Pressure Gauge
Calibrated Stopwatch
Calibrated Water Collection Vessel
Calibrated Flow Meter
Bucket

	USP WATER SYSTEM OPERATIONAL QUALIFICATION PROTOCOL		Page 6 of 24
Protocol No.: Relate to IQ	Effective Date:	Revision No.: 0	Supersedes: N/A

2.4   TEST EQUIPMENT DATA SHEET

List all test equipment, ID numbers and calibration due dates. All instruments and equipment should be within current calibration, and the calibrations should be traceable to NIST (National Institute of Standards and Technology) standards. Calibrated Process instrumentation may be used in place of external test equipment when appropriate.

TEST EQUIPMENT	ID NUMBER	LAST CALIBRATION DATE	CALIBRATION DUE DATE

COMMENTS:_____

_____
_____
_____
_____
_____
_____
_____
_____
_____
_____
_____
_____
_____
_____

	USP WATER SYSTEM OPERATIONAL QUALIFICATION PROTOCOL		Page 7 of 24
Protocol No.: Relate to IQ	Effective Date:	Revision No.: 0	Supersedes: N/A

3.0   EXECUTION

The following Operational Qualification sections will detail the documentation required to verify that the operation of the USP Water System adheres to the design specifications.

3.1   OPERATIONAL PREREQUISITES

Verify that the following prerequisites are complete prior to initiating this protocol.

PREREQUISITE	INITIALS	DATE
The Installation Qualification of the USP Water System has been completed and approved.		
Verification that all instrumentation necessary for the execution of this protocol have been or will be calibrated prior to use		

COMMENTS: _____

_____
_____
_____
_____
_____
_____
_____
_____
_____
_____
_____
_____
_____
_____

Conducted By: _____   Date: _____

Reviewed By: _____   Date: _____

	USP WATER SYSTEM OPERATIONAL QUALIFICATION PROTOCOL		Page 8 of 24	
Protocol No.: Relate to IQ	Effective Date:		Revision No.: 0	Supersedes: N/A

4.0 OPERATIONAL QUALIFICATION

The following Operational Qualification sections will verify and document that the USP Water System operates in a manner consistent with design specifications.

4.1 OPERATING INSTRUCTION PROCEDURE VERIFICATION

TITLE	Number	REV	Date	Yes/No	By/Date
The following SOPs for the USP Water System exist and are current					
Servicing the USP Purified Water System					
USP Purified Water Monitoring Program					
Sanitization of the USP Purified Water Distribution System					
Dispensing USP Purified Water from the USP Water Distribution System					

COMMENTS: _____
_____
_____
_____
_____
_____
_____
_____

Conducted By: _____   Date: _____

Reviewed By: _____   Date: _____

	USP WATER SYSTEM OPERATIONAL QUALIFICATION PROTOCOL		Page 9 of 24
Protocol No.: Relate to IQ	Effective Date:	Revision No.: 0	Supersedes: N/A

4.2   EQUIPMENT LOGS

The following logs are used to document the usage, equipment cleaning and equipment maintenance. Verify that the logs are complete and current.

Log Title	Log Number	Log Location	Log Current (Yes/No)

COMMENTS: _____
_____
_____
_____
_____
_____
_____
_____
_____
_____

Conducted By: _____   Date: _____

Reviewed By: _____   Date: _____

	USP WATER SYSTEM OPERATIONAL QUALIFICATION PROTOCOL		Page 10 of 24
Protocol No.: Relate to IQ	Effective Date:	Revision No.: 0	Supersedes: N/A

4.3   ULTRAVIOLET LAMP

Operational Testing	Yes/No	Performed By	Date
UV sterilizer has been operational for a minimum period of 15 minutes.			
The point of use valve is open.			
Running time meter is operational.			
All LED indicators on the operational display panel are illuminated.			
When the UV lamp is inoperative, the corresponding LED indicator on the operational display panel is extinguished.			
Disconnect the power to the UV sterilizer.			
Remove the lamp from the UV sterilizer.			
Reconnect the power to the UV sterilizer.			
The UV lamp LED indicator is extinguished.			
The point of use valve closes.			
Record the UV lamp intensity after restarting			

COMMENTS: _____
_____
_____
_____
_____
_____
_____
_____
_____

Conducted By: _____   Date: _____

Reviewed By: _____   Date: _____

	USP WATER SYSTEM OPERATIONAL QUALIFICATION PROTOCOL		Page 11 of 24
Protocol No.: Relate to IQ	Effective Date:	Revision No.: 0	Supersedes: N/A

4.4 PUMP CAPACITY

Testing Procedure

1. Record the pump ID, impeller size and motor size (HP) on the appropriate form.

2. Measure inlet and outlet pressures at the pump and record on the appropriate form.

3. Using the pump curve of the pump, motor and impeller being tested, calculate the discharge flowrate and record on the appropriate form.

4. Repeat the test three (3) times at least 1 hour apart.

Acceptance Criteria

The actual pump flowrate is within the pump curve flowrate.

	USP WATER SYSTEM OPERATIONAL QUALIFICATION PROTOCOL		Page 12 of 24
Protocol No.: Relate to IQ	Effective Date:	Revision No.: 0	Supersedes: N/A

4.5   PUMP CAPACITY VERIFICATION (Cont.)

4.5.1   USP Water Generation Package

USP Water Generation Package Pump			
Pump ID			
Impeller Size (in)			
Motor Size (HP)			
Trial #	**1/Time**	**2/Time**	**3/Time**
Pump Inlet Pressure (psig)			
Pump Outlet Pressure (psig)			
Calculated Flowrate (gpm) from Pump Curve			
Calculate Flowrate ≥ 10% of Measured Flowrate			
Pass/Fail			
Initials/Date			

COMMENTS: _____
_____
_____
_____
_____
_____
_____

Conducted By: _____   Date: _____

Reviewed By: _____   Date: _____

	USP WATER SYSTEM OPERATIONAL QUALIFICATION PROTOCOL		Page 13 of 24
Protocol No.: Relate to IQ	Effective Date:	Revision No.: 0	Supersedes: N/A

PUMP CAPACITY VERIFICATION (Cont.)

      4.5.2   USP Water Distribution Pump

USP Water Pump			
Pump ID			
Impeller Size (in)			
Motor Size (HP)			
Trial #	**1/Time**	**2/Time**	**3/Time**
Pump Inlet Pressure (psig)			
Pump Outlet Pressure (psig)			
Calculated Flowrate (gpm) from Pump Curve			
Calculate Flowrate ≥ 10% of Measured Flowrate			
Pass/Fail			
Initials/Date			

COMMENTS: _____
_____
_____
_____
_____
_____
_____

Conducted By: _____   Date: _____

Reviewed By: _____   Date: _____

	USP WATER SYSTEM OPERATIONAL QUALIFICATION PROTOCOL		Page 14 of 24
Protocol No.: Relate to IQ	Effective Date:	Revision No.: 0	Supersedes: N/A

4.5   TEMPERATURE REQUIREMENTS VERIFICATION

Testing Procedure

1.   The purpose of this test is to verify that the Water for Operation System meets the requirements specified by the manufacturer and COMPANY.

2.   Water temperatures (for information only) will be recorded from the following:

- USP Water Generation Package outlet.
- USP Water distribution loops.
- USP Water recirculation loop.

3.   Record the water temperatures on the appropriate data sheet from the specified locations during "no load" and maximum load conditions.

Acceptance Criteria

Recorded temperatures must be within ± 5% of the manufacturer and COMPANY specified temperatures.

Location	Line Number	Specified Temperature (°C)	"No Load" Temperature (°C)	"Max Load" Temperature (°C)
USP Water Generation Package Outlet				
USP Water Distribution Loop Inlet.				
USP Water Distribution Loop Return				

COMMENTS: _____

_____

_____

_____

Conducted By: _____   Date: _____

Reviewed By: _____   Date: _____

	USP WATER SYSTEM OPERATIONAL QUALIFICATION PROTOCOL		Page 15 of 24	
Protocol No.: Relate to IQ	Effective Date:	Revision No.: 0	Supersedes: N/A	

4.6 ALARMS AND INTERLOCKS

Verify that for the Alarm Interlock System of the USP Water System the expected responses are obtained.

Alarm/Interlock	Expected Response	Actual Response	Initials	Date

COMMENTS: _____

_____

_____

_____

_____

_____

_____

_____

_____

_____

_____

Conducted By: _____ Date: _____

Reviewed By: _____ Date: _____

	USP WATER SYSTEM OPERATIONAL QUALIFICATION PROTOCOL		Page 16 of 27
Protocol No.: Relate to IQ	Effective Date:	Revision No.: 0	Supersedes: N/A

4.7 SYSTEM CLEANING VERIFICATION

Testing Procedure

1. The purpose of the system cleaning verification is to demonstrate that the USP Water System can be adequately cleaned and that the system can be flushed to return the original USP Purified Water quality.

2. The water system will be cleaned using the written procedures that are provided (refer SOP ML-WS03).

3. The test procedure for cleaning the USP Water System is to observe the cleaning of the system by trained operators and to record the performance of the cleaning procedure on the appropriate forms.

Acceptance Criteria

1. The procedures in place are according to manufacturer or Company recommended exposure time and concentration (SOP ML-WS03).

2. All lines and components have had adequate flushing.

3. After the cleaning procedure, the water system generates USP purified grade water.

	USP WATER SYSTEM OPERATIONAL QUALIFICATION PROTOCOL		Page 17 of 24
Protocol No.: Relate to IQ	Effective Date:	Revision No.: 0	Supersedes: N/A

4.7 SYSTEM CLEANING VERIFICATION (Cont.)

4.9.1   USP Water Generation Package

System Sanitation Operation Test Data Sheet

Cleaning Procedure Start Time: _____

Cleaning procedure End Time: _____

Sanitizing Solution _____

Sanitizing Temperature/Flow rate _____/_____

Criteria	Results Acceptable (Yes/No)	Initials	Date
Procedures are in place to properly sanitize the water system.			
Proper level of Minncare for sanitation is obtained.			
Adequate time at concentration for sanitation.			
All ports have had adequate flushing.			
All points of use ports have achieved adequate levels of sanitation solution. Test strips turn black. (Test with 1% Minncare TS)			
Post sanitation flushing reduces sanitation solution to less than _____ ppm of Minncare.			

COMMENTS: _____
_____
_____
_____
_____
_____
_____
_____

Conducted By: _____   Date: _____

Reviewed By: _____   Date: _____

	USP WATER SYSTEM OPERATIONAL QUALIFICATION PROTOCOL		Page 18 of 24
Protocol No.: .: Relate to IQ	Effective Date:	Revision No.: 0	Supersedes: N/A

4.7 SYSTEM CLEANING VERIFICATION (Cont.)

    4.7.1   USP Water Distribution Loops

    System Sanitation Operation Test Data Sheet

    Cleaning Procedure Start Time: _____

    Cleaning procedure End Time: _____

    Sanitizing Solution _____

    Sanitizing Temperature/Flow rate _____/_____

Criteria	Results Acceptable (Yes/No)	Initials	Date
Procedures are in place to properly sanitize the water system.			
Proper level of Minncare for sanitation is obtained.			
Adequate time at concentration for sanitation.			
All ports have had adequate flushing.			
All points of use ports have achieved adequate levels of sanitation solution. Test strips turn black. (Test with 1% Minncare TS)			
Post sanitation flushing reduces sanitation solution to less than _____ ppm of Minncare			

COMMENTS: _____

_____

_____

_____

_____

_____

_____

_____

Conducted By: _____   Date: _____

Reviewed By: _____   Date: _____

	USP WATER SYSTEM OPERATIONAL QUALIFICATION PROTOCOL		Page 19 of 24
Protocol No.: .: Relate to IQ	Effective Date:	Revision No.: 0	Supersedes: N/A

4.8 SYSTEM CAPACITY VERIFICATION

Testing Procedure

1. The purpose of the system capacity verification is to demonstrate that the USP Water System meets capacity requirements within the manufacturer and COMPANY specifications.

2. The capacity of the USP Water System will be tested in order to verify that the system can deliver the required amount of water to the maximum number of points of use that will be open at any given time during normal operation.

3. Record the flowrate measured from the output of the water distribution pump, which feeds the water distribution loops, on the appropriate data sheet.

4. Record the flowrate of the water generated from the USP Water Generation Package on the appropriate data sheet.

Acceptance Criteria

The expected output volumes are within ± _____ % of the required output volumes.

Description	Expected Output (gpm)	Actual Output (gpm)	Initials	Date
USP Water Generation Package				

COMMENTS: _____
_____
_____
_____
_____
_____

Conducted By: _____   Date: _____

Reviewed By: _____   Date: _____

	USP WATER SYSTEM OPERATIONAL QUALIFICATION PROTOCOL		Page 20 of 24	
Protocol No.: Relate to IQ	Effective Date:		Revision No.: 0	Supersedes: N/A

4.9 COMPUTER SYSTEMS VERIFICATION
Testing Procedure

1. The purpose of the computer system verification is to verify the proper operation of the Programmable Logic Controller. The following test will be performed:
   - System Backup
   - System power Loss Recovery
   - Radio Frequency and Electromagnetic Interference (RFI & EMI)
2. System Backup – Verify that there is an offline copy of the software that runs the USP Water Generation Package and that it is stored in a secure location.
3. Verify that there is a procedure to restore the program into the Programmable Logic Controller should there be a total program loss in the system memory.
4. System Power Loss – Simulate a power loss to the USP Water Generation Package control panel. Verify that the operational system can be restarted following a power loss.
5. Radio Frequency Interference (RFI) and Electromagnetic Interference (EMI) – At separate times, operate a maintenance walkie-talkie and a hand drill in the immediate area of the USP Water control panel. Document on the data sheet that the RFI and EMI sources have no effect on the operation of the USP Water control system.
6. Reference any control system verification executed on the USP Water Generation Package during SAT/Commissioning and Startup verifications.
7. Reference system backup, system power loss, RFI & EMI and any control system verification executed on the USP Water Distribution Loops, performed during SAT/Commissioning, Startup and qualification verifications.

USP Water Generation Package Control System

Description	Expected Response	Actual Response	Initials	Date
Computer System Backup	Offline copy of the program can be uploaded to the resident controller.			
Computer System Recovery	System can be restarted following a power failure.			
RFI Interference – within 3 Ft of unit (all sides)	No effect on system operation.			
EMI Interference within 3 Ft of unit (all sides	No effect on system operation.			

Conducted By: _____   Date: _____

Reviewed By: _____   Date: _____

	USP WATER SYSTEM OPERATIONAL QUALIFICATION PROTOCOL		Page 21 of 24
Protocol No.: Relate to IQ	Effective Date:	Revision No.: 0	Supersedes: N/A

4.10   DAILY OPERATIONAL CHECKOUT

The purpose of the daily operational checkout is to document the proper operation of the USP Water (USP) System, as per manufacturer and COMPANY requirements. The procedure for the daily operational checkout is the following:

Observe the operation of the USP System for a period of one week and document on the data sheet the operational characteristics of the system. These operational parameters should remain relatively constant, in accordance with the manufacturer's manual.

Parameter	Mon	Tues	Wed	Thurs	Fri	Sat	Sun

COMMENTS: _____

_____

_____

_____

_____

_____

_____

Conducted By: _____   Date: _____

Reviewed By: _____   Date: _____

	USP WATER SYSTEM OPERATIONAL QUALIFICATION PROTOCOL		Page 22 of 24
Protocol No.: Relate to IQ	Effective Date:	Revision No.: 0	Supersedes: N/A

4.11   EXCEPTIONAL CONDITIONS

Discrepancies may be observed as the protocol is being executed. Should this occur, an "Exceptional Condition Report" is to be prepared. The exceptional Condition Report" is to identify the discrepancy found, project the impact, and suggest recommendations. In conjunction with COMPANY, a plan of action will be determined and an appropriate corrective action taken.

EXCEPTIONAL CONDITION REPORT

Date: _____   # _____

Discrepancy:
_____
_____
_____
_____

Impact:
_____
_____
_____
_____

Recommendations:
_____
_____
_____
_____

Corrective Action: No.: _____
_____
_____
_____
_____

____ Critical Deviation   ____ Non-Critical Deviation

QA Assessed By: _____   Date: _____

State reason why Deviation is classifies as non-critical: _____
_____

Satisfactorily Completed (Y/N): _____

Conducted By: _____   Date: _____

Reviewed By: _____   Date: _____

	USP WATER SYSTEM OPERATIONAL QUALIFICATION PROTOCOL		Page 23 of 24
Protocol No.: Relate to IQ	Effective Date:	Revision No.: 0	Supersedes: N/A

5.0 FINAL REPORT STATEMENT

A final report will be written after the execution of the IQ, OQ, and PQ (if necessary). The contents of the report, along with the protocol, will contain all data relevant to this qualification. The report will also include Exceptional Conditions found along with the applicable resolutions. The report will be reviewed and signed by the pertinent Validation Support Team members and the Validation Manager. The final report and the protocol will be used for certification of the equipment / system.

	USP WATER SYSTEM OPERATIONAL QUALIFICATION PROTOCOL		Page 24 of 24
Protocol No.: .: Relate to IQ	Effective Date:	Revision No.: 0	Supersedes: N/A

6.0 FINAL APPROVAL SIGNATURES

Final approval signifies concurrence that protocol criteria has been satisfactorily addressed per COMPANY specifications and intended use, and that all deviations and/or discrepancies have been resolved.

USP Water System
Operational Qualification Protocol
Protocol Number:

PROTOCOL REVIEWED BY: _____ DATE: _____

PROTOCOL APPROVED BY:

VALIDATION: _____ DATE: _____
COMPANY

ENGINEERING: _____ DATE: _____
COMPANY

ENGINEERING: _____ DATE: _____
COMPANY

QA: _____ DATE: _____
COMPANY

PROTOCOL APPROVAL SIGNIFIES CONCURRENCE WITH THE TESTS, PROCEDURES, AND ACCEPTANCE CRITERIA OUTLINED HEREIN.

Performance Qualification Protocol
for the
USP Water System

PREPARED FOR:

Company
City, State

PREPARED BY:
XXXXXXXXX
City, State

Protocol No.:
Revision No.: 0
Date:

TABLE OF CONTENTS

	USP WATER SYSTEM INSTALLATION QUALIFICATION PROTOCOL		Page 4 of 21
Protocol No.:	Effective Date:	Revision No.: 0	Supersedes: None

Revision Record

Revision	Date	Changes
A		Draft
0		Original

Reviewed By: _____   Date: _____

	USP WATER SYSTEM INSTALLATION QUALIFICATION PROTOCOL		Page 5 of 21
Protocol No.:	Effective Date:	Revision No.: 0	Supersedes: None

USP Water System
Performance Qualification Protocol
Protocol Number:

PROTOCOL PREPARED BY: _____ DATE: _____
                                                       Signature
                                              Print_____

PROTOCOL APPROVED BY:

VALIDATION: _____ DATE: _____
                                    COMPANY
                                    Signature
                            Print_____

ENGINEERING: _____ DATE:_____
                                    COMPANY
                                    Signature
                            Print_____

OPERATIONS: _____ DATE:_____
                                    COMPANY
                                    Signature
                            Print_____

QC LABORATORY: _____ DATE:_____
                                    COMPANY
                                    Signature
                            Print_____

QA: _____ DATE: _____
                            COMPANY
                            Signature
                    Print_____

PROTOCOL APPROVAL SIGNIFIES CONCURRENCE WITH THE TESTS, PROCEDURES AND
ACCEPTANCE CRITERIA OUTLINED HEREIN.

Reviewed By: _____   Date: _____

	USP WATER SYSTEM INSTALLATION QUALIFICATION PROTOCOL		Page 6 of 21
Protocol No.:	Effective Date:	Revision No.: 0	Supersedes: None

1.0 GENERAL

This protocol defines the Performance Qualification (PQ) requirements and the corresponding acceptance criteria for a USP Purified Water System located at the COMPANY, Inc. located in City, State

2.0 SYSTEM/EQUIPMENT DESCRIPTION

2.1 GENERAL

The USP Water System is comprised of two distribution loops, which supply water to the production areas of the building. Refer to drawing and block diagram below.

The system has an in-line TOC monitor and a conductivity meter. There is a UV light at 185 nm to target TOC distribution and another UV light at 254 nm to target biological distribution. The control system provides warning and shutdown alarms. The USP Water System is comprised of the following components:

        Carbon Bed Filter
        Ultraviolet Light (254nm)
        Pump
        3 Mixed bed Ion Exchange Units
        Filter Units
        USP Distribution Loops
        USP 316L SS Distribution Loop

2.2 System Block Diagram

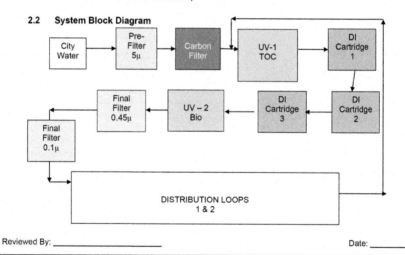

Reviewed By: _____   Date: _____

	USP WATER SYSTEM INSTALLATION QUALIFICATION PROTOCOL		Page 7 of 21
Protocol No.:	Effective Date:	Revision No.: 0	Supersedes: None

2.3   RECOMMENDED VALIDATION EQUIPMENT

Validation equipment that may be required for the execution of this protocol includes, but is not limited to:

> Sterile Sample Containers
> Gloves

2.4   TEST EQUIPMENT DATA

List all instruments and equipment used in the testing of the   USP Water System, their identification numbers and calibration due dates. All instruments and equipment should be within current calibration, and the calibrations should be traceable to NIST (National Institute of Standards and Technology) standards.   Calibrated USP generation skid and/or PCS instrumentation will be used in place of external test equipment where appropriate.

Test Equipment	ID Number	Last Calibration Date	Calibration Due Date

COMMENTS: _____

_____

_____

Reviewed By: _____   Date: _____

	USP WATER SYSTEM INSTALLATION QUALIFICATION PROTOCOL		Page 8 of 21
Protocol No.:	Effective Date:	Revision No.: 0	Supersedes: None

3.0   PROCEDURE

The following Performance Qualification sections will detail the documentation required to verify that the operation of the USP Water System adheres to Company specifications of.:

3.1   OPERATIONAL PREREQUISITES

Verify that the following prerequisites are complete prior to initiating this protocol.

PREREQUISITE	INITIALS	DATE
The Installation Qualification of the USP Water System has been completed and approved.		
The Operation Qualification protocols for the USP Water System are complete and all exceptional conditions have been resolved.		
Verification that all instrumentation necessary for the execution of this protocol have been calibrated and are in current calibration.		

COMMENTS:_____
_____
_____
_____
_____
_____
_____
_____
_____
_____
_____

Reviewed By: _____   Date: _____

	USP WATER SYSTEM INSTALLATION QUALIFICATION PROTOCOL		Page 9 of 21
Protocol No.:	Effective Date:	Revision No.: 0	Supersedes: None

3.2   WATER SAMPLING PLAN

3.2.1   This water sampling plan describes the sample locations, the samples that will be taken, the frequency of the sampling, the tests to be performed on the samples, and the acceptance criteria for the sample tests. The water-sampling plan will detail a two-phase water quality-monitoring program that will be used to qualify the Water System.

3.2.2   Phase I consists of two weeks of intensive daily water quality monitoring. At completion of Phase I, validation field reports will be completed.

3.2.3   All ports are tested daily to demonstrate that the operational protocols are adequate.

3.2.4   Phase II begins at the completion of Phase I. Phase II has a duration of four (4) weeks of intensive water quality monitoring.

3.2.5   Phase III begins at the completion of Phase II and a duration of one (1) year. Any variations in the water quality over an extended period of time will be revealed during Phase III. The sampling plan for Phase III will align with COMPANY's routine sampling procedure as specified in SOP XXXXX. Phase III confirms that the USP Water System is able to accommodate seasonal variation in the water supply.

3.2.6   Throughout the execution of the PQ protocol, the water system will be operated in accordance with COMPANY internal SOP(s). As a part of those SOP(s), a "USP Water System Daily Operating Log" will be completed. This log will give an indication of the operational characteristics of the system during the PQ testing. A copy of the log will be attached to the completed protocol.

3.2.7   The USP Water System may be used "at risk," for manufacturing, if data obtained during the first full week of testing is determined to be appropriate.

Reviewed By: _____   Date: _____

	USP WATER SYSTEM INSTALLATION QUALIFICATION PROTOCOL		Page 10 of 21
Protocol No.:	Effective Date:	Revision No.: 0	Supersedes: None

3.2   WATER SAMPLING PLAN Continued

<u>Water Sample Test Plan – Sample Locations</u>

Sample Point	Location / Title
1	After filter
2	After Carbon bed Filter
3	After UV light-
4	After Mix bed
5	After Mix bed
6	After UV light -
7	After filter
8	Use point 6
9	Use Point 8
10	Use Point 18
11	Use Point 24
12	Use Point 25
13	Use Point 26
14	Use Point 27
15	Use Point 28
16	Use Point 29
17	Use Point 30
18	Use Point 31
19	Use Point 32

Reviewed By: _____   Date: _____

	USP WATER SYSTEM INSTALLATION QUALIFICATION PROTOCOL		Page 11 of 21
Protocol No.:	Effective Date:	Revision No.: 0	Supersedes: None

3.2 WATER SAMPLING PLAN Continued

3.2.8 Sample Collection and Analysis

3.2.8.1 Refer to the sampling chart on pages 11 and 12 for a description of the sampling schedule, sampling locations and laboratory tests to be performed. Phase I testing is two weeks. Phase II testing is 4 weeks and Phase III samples each point according to COMPANY SOP for one year.

3.2.8.2 Prepare the "Sample Collection Data Sheet" for each day of water system sampling.

3.2.8.3 Use Company's SOP Prep/Filling XXXX for sampling procedures.

3.2.8.4 Record all water sample tests results on the "Water Sample Test Results Data Sheet".

3.2.8.5 Ensure that the water system is operated in accordance with COMPANY SOPs (refer to IQ SOP List) and that a "USP Water System Daily Operating Log" has been completed for the days in test. Attach a copy of the completed log to the "Water Sample Test Results Data Sheet."

3.2.8.6 Ensure that the completion of system sanitization report is attached.

Reviewed By: _____   Date: _____

	USP WATER SYSTEM INSTALLATION QUALIFICATION PROTOCOL		Page 12 of 21
Protocol No.:	Effective Date:	Revision No.: 0	Supersedes: None

3.2 WATER SAMPLING PLAN Continued

USP Water Sampling Plan
Phase I – Weeks 1, & 2

Sample Point	Sampling Days and Tests						
	Monday	Tuesday	Wednesday	Thursday	Friday	Saturday	Sunday
1	M	M	M	M	M	M	M
2	M	C, M	M	C, M	M	M	M
3	M	M	M	M	C, M	M	M
4	M	M	C, M	M	M	C, M	M
5	C, M	C, M	C, M	C, M	C, M	C, M	C, M
6	C, M	M	M	M	M	M	M
7	C,M	C,M	C,M	C,M	C,M	C,M	C,M
8	C,M	M	M	M	M	M	M
9	M	C,M	M	C,M	M	M	M
10	M	M	M	M	C,M	M	M
11	M	M	C,M	M	M	C,M	M
12	M	M	M	M	M	M	C,M
13	C,M	M	M	M	M	M	M
14	M	C,M	M	C,M	M	M	M
15	M	M	M	M	C,M	M	M
16	TOC	TOC	TOC	TOC	TOC	TOC	TOC
17	TOC	TOC	TOC	TOC	TOC	TOC	TOC
18	Cond.	Cond	Cond	Cond	Cond	Cond	Cond

C = Chemical or TOC = Total Organic Carbon, Cond = Conductivity, M = Microbiological, T = Temperature

Reviewed By: _____ Date: _____

USP WATER SYSTEM INSTALLATION QUALIFICATION PROTOCOL			Page 13 of 21
Protocol No.:	Effective Date:	Revision No.: 0	Supersedes: None

3.2 WATER SAMPLING PLAN Continued

USP Water Sampling Plan
Phase II

Sampling Points	DAY 1	2	3	4	5	6	7	8	9	10	11	12	13	14	15	16	17	18	19	20	21	22	23	24	25	26	27	28
1	1															1												
2		1															1											
3			1			1																	1					
4				1				1		1														1				
5		3	3	3	3			3	3	3	3	3			3	3	3	3	3			3	3	3	3			
6		3	3	3	3			3	3	3	3	3			3	3	3	3	3			3	3	3	3			
7		2	2	2	2			2	2	2	2	2			2	2	2	2	2			2	2	2	2			
8		2	2	2	2			2	2	2	2	2			2	2	2	2	2			2	2	2	2			
9		3	3	3	3			3	3	3	3	3			3	3	3	3	3			3	3	3	3			
10		2	2	2	2			2	2	2	2	2			2	2	2	2	2			2	2	2	2			
11		2	2	2	2			2	2	2	2	2			2	2	2	2	2			2	2	2	2			

1 = Chemical, Bacterial Endotoxins, Microbiological; 2 = Conductivity, 3 = Total Organic Carbon, 4 = Temperature

3.3   WATER SAMPLING PLAN Continued
USP Water Sampling Plan
Phase II

Sampling Points	DAY																											
	1	2	3	4	5	6	7	8	9	10	11	12	13	14	15	16	17	18	19	20	21	22	23	24	25	26	27	28
12	1																											
13		1							1							1							1					
14			1							1							1							1				
15				1							1							1							1			
16	3	3	3	3	3			3	3	3	3	3			3	3	3	3	3			3	3	3	3	3		
17	3	3	3	3	3			3	3	3	3	3			3	3	3	3	3			3	3	3	3	3		
18	2	2	2	2	2			2	2	2	2	2			2	2	2	2	2			2	2	2	2	2		
19	2	2	2	2	2			2	2	2	2	2			2	2	2	2	2			2	2	2	2	2		
20	4	4	4	4	4			4	4	4	4	4			4	4	4	4	4			4	4	4	4	4		
21	4	4	4	4	4			4	4	4	4	4			4	4	4	4	4			4	4	4	4	4		
22	4	4	4	4	4			4	4	4	4	4			4	4	4	4	4			4	4	4	4	4		

1 = Chemical, Bacterial Endotoxins, Microbiological;   2 = Resistivity,   3 = Total Organic Carbon,   4 = Temperature

Reviewed By: _____

Date: _____

3.3   ACCEPTANCE CRITERIA

3.3.1 Microbiological Analysis

3.3.1.1 A certificate of analysis from the manufacturer must accompany each lot of medium used for testing water samples.

3.3.1.2 Microbiological testing will be in accordance with COMPANY's SOP XXXXX

3.3.1.3 Feed Water must comply with federal regulations (41 CFR) for drinking water with respect to bacteriological purity.

3.3.1.4 Refer to Company XXXXXXX which states limits of:

-

3.4   SAMPLE COLLECTION DATA SHEET

WATER SAMPLE SCHEDULE DATA SHEET

Phase: _____   Week: _____   Sample Date: _____   Page ___ of ___

Sample Point	Location	Sample ID	Tests Ordered*	Verified By/Date

Cond = Conductivity,   M = Microbiological, TOC = Total Organic Carbon,   T = Temperature

COMMENTS:_____
_____
_____
_____

	USP WATER SYSTEM INSTALLATION QUALIFICATION PROTOCOL	Page 16 of 21
Protocol No.:	Effective Date:	Revision No.: 0	Protocol No.:

3.5   FIELD VERIFICATION DATA SHEET

PQ FIELD VERIFICATION

Description	Yes / No	Phase / Date Occurred	Verified By	Date
Daily operational log sheet completed.				
Daily usage of the USP Purified Water System documented.				
USP Purified Water System shutdown challenge performed.				
Cleaning of the USP Purified Water System occurred.				

COMMENTS:_____

_____
_____
_____
_____
_____
_____
_____
_____
_____
_____
_____
_____
_____
_____
_____
_____
_____

Reviewed By: _____   Date: _____

	USP WATER SYSTEM INSTALLATION QUALIFICATION PROTOCOL		Page 17 of 21
Protocol No.:	Effective Date:	Revision No.: 0	Protocol No.:

3.6   LABORATORY REPORT SHEET

WATER SAMPLE TEST RESULTS

Phase: _____   Week: _____   Sample Date: _____   Page ___ of ___

Sample Point	Bioburden Results Pass / Fail	Conductivity Results	TOC	Verified By / Date

COMMENTS: Limits -
Conductivity_____
TOC_____
Bioburden_____
Temperature – For monitoring only – no limit_____
_____

Reviewed By: _____   Date: _____

	USP WATER SYSTEM INSTALLATION QUALIFICATION PROTOCOL		Page 18 of 21
Protocol No.:	Effective Date:	Revision No.: 0	Protocol No.:

3.7   EXCEPTIONAL CONDITIONS

Discrepancies may be observed as the protocol is being executed. Should this occur, an "Exceptional Condition Report" is to be prepared. The Exceptional Condition Report" is to identify the discrepancy found, project the impact, and suggest recommendations. In conjunction with COMPANY, a plan of action will be determined and an appropriate corrective action taken.

EXCEPTIONAL CONDITION REPORT

Date: _____   # _____

Assessed By QA   _____   Date _____

Discrepancy:

_____
_____
_____
_____
_____

Impact:

_____
_____
_____
_____
_____

Recommendations:

_____
_____
_____
_____
_____

Corrective Action: No.: _____

_____
_____
_____

_____ **Critical Deviation**   _____ **Non-Critical Deviation**

State reason why Deviation is classifies as non-critical: _____

_____

Satisfactorily Completed (Y/N): _____

Reviewed By: _____   Date: _____

	USP WATER SYSTEM INSTALLATION QUALIFICATION PROTOCOL		Page 19 of 21
Protocol No.:	Effective Date:	Revision No.: 0	Protocol No.:

4.0   FINAL REPORT STATEMENT

A final report will be written after the execution of the IQ, OQ and PQ. The contents of the report, along with the protocols, will contain all data relevant to this qualification. The report will also include Exceptional Conditions found along with the applicable resolutions. The report will be reviewed and signed by the pertinent Validation Support Team members, the Validation Manager, and Senior Quality Management. The final report and the protocols will be used for certification of the water system.

	USP WATER SYSTEM PERFORMANCE QUALIFICATION PROTOCOL		Page 20 of 21
Protocol No.:	Effective Date:	Revision No.: A	Supersedes: N/A

5.0   FINAL APPROVAL SIGNATURES

Final approval signifies concurrence that protocol criteria have been satisfactorily addressed per COMPANY specifications and intended use, and that all deviations and/or discrepancies have been resolved.

**USP Water System
Performance Qualification Protocol
Protocol Number:**

PROTOCOL APPROVED BY:

VALIDATION: _____ DATE: _____
                                                COMPANY
                                                Signature
                                Print_____

ENGINEERING: _____ DATE:_____
                                                COMPANY
                                                Signature
                                Print_____

OPERATIONS: _____ DATE:_____
                                                COMPANY
                                                Signature
                                Print_____

QC LABORATORY: _____ DATE:_____
                                                COMPANY
                                                Signature
                                Print_____

QA: _____ DATE: _____
                                                COMPANY
                                                Signature
                                Print_____

PROTOCOL APPROVAL SIGNIFIES CONCURRENCE WITH THE TESTS, PROCEDURES AND ACCEPTANCE CRITERIA OUTLINED HEREIN.

SHELF DRYER SYSTEM
I/O/PQ PROTOCOL

PREPARED FOR:
COMPANY

Document No.: XXX-XX-X_XXXXX
Date:

	Title: Shelf Dryer System IO/PQ Protocol
	Document #: XXX-XX-X_XXXXX
	Revision Date:
	Page 2 of 38

TABLE OF CONTENTS

	Title: Shelf Dryer System IO/PQ Protocol	
	Document #: XXX-XX-X_XXXXX	
	Revision Date:	
		Page 3 of 38

Shelf Dryer System (XX) Validation Protocol

Protocol Objective: This qualification will provide documented verification that key aspects of the Shelf Dryer System (XX) and its installation, operation and performance adhere to the design specifications. Additionally, this protocol will provide a baseline of installation, operational and performance data to serve as a reference for change control in the future.

Protocol Scope: This study will be performed on the Shelf Dryer System (XX). This protocol defines the test procedures, documentation, references and acceptance criteria used to establish that the system is installed and operates properly in accordance with the applicable specifications and intended use. The executed protocol will verify that all installation, operational and performance acceptance criteria have been met, and that the Shelf Dryer System (XX) meets current Good Manufacturing Practice (cGMP) requirements.

PROTOCOL PREPARED BY: _____   DATE: _____
                               Name
                               Company

PROTOCOL REVIEWED BY: _____   DATE: _____
                               Name
                               Company

APPROVED BY:

Process   _____   DATE: _____
                               Name
                               Company

Engineering   _____   DATE: _____
                               Name
                               Company

R & D_____   DATE: _____
                               Name
                               Company

QA._____   Date_____
                               Name
                               Company

	Title: Shelf Dryer System IO/PQ Protocol
	Document #: XXX-XX-X_XXXXX
	Revision Date:
	Page 4 of 38

1.0 PROTOCOL OVERVIEW

1.1   Protocol Manager

1.2   Validation Team

1.3   Shelf Dryer System Description
General:

The Shelf Dryer System, XX, consists of a x sq. ft., jacketed, stainless steel vacuum shelf dryer XXX, a dedicated temperature control unit (TCU), XXX, consisting of an electric heater, a shell and tube cooler, an expansion tank, and a circulating pump, a two-stage dryer discharge HEPA filter, XXX, and a Nitrogen filter, XXX. The dryer heating and cooling medium is 50% propylene glycol.

Dryer vacuum is provided by the U-XX-x. Vent to the vacuum system passes through Nitrogen Filter, XXX rated at 0.3 micron.

Dryer Temperature Control:

Temperature control of the dryer system is enabled by starting of the dryer TCU circulating pump from the PCS at XXX-XX-x. The local "Hand-Off-Auto" (HOA) selector at the circulating pump, XXX-XXX-x, must be in the "AUTO" position to enable control of the system from the PCS. .

When the local "HOA" selector is in the "HAND" position, the pump will start but there will be no PCS functionality available.

When the system is stopped from the PCS at XXX-XXX-x, the temperature controller, XXX-XXX-x is placed into manual mode with setpoint tracking enabled, and the output is set to x% to turn off the electric heater.

Circulation Pump Control:

As mentioned, the circulation pump, (as well as the dryer temperature control loop), is normally started from the PCS through xxxxxxxx with the local "Hand/Off/Auto" selector, XXX-XXX-x in the "Auto" position. The dryer circulation pump may be started locally at the pump with XXX-XXX-x in the "Hand" position. Temperature control of the dryer is not available in this case.

In either case, an auxiliary motor contact provides a motor run feedback to the PCS at XXX-XXX-x. This provides run confirmation for enabling a color change of the pump icon on the operator screen. As there is no feedback available from the HOA,

	Title: Shelf Dryer System IO/PQ Protocol
	Document #: XXX-XX-X_XXXXX
	Revision Date:
	Page 5 of 38

command logic in the PCS determines whether the pump has been started locally or from the PCS. The pump icon color will differ as a result of this logic.

A transition time is configured into the software to allow an approximate 5 second, (adjustable), delay for the circulation pump to start and provide the confirming motor contact feedback, XXX-XXX-x. Failure to start in this time frame will generate an alarm.

Chilled Water Isolation Valve:

XXX-XXX-x on the chilled water supply to the dryer cooler will open on command from the system mode selector switch, XXX-XXX-x, when placed in the "Cool" position.

Shelf Dryer Vacuum Control:

A pressure transmitter, XXX-XXX-x on the vent line to the vacuum pump system provides an input to the PCS at XXX-XXX-x, which in turn sends a modulating analog output to the vacuum control valve, XXX-XXX-x. Dryer vacuum is provided on the operator screen at XXX-XXX-x.

	Title: Shelf Dryer System
	IO/PQ Protocol
	Document #: XXX-XX-X_XXXXX
	Revision Date:
	Page 6 of 38

2.0   INSTALLATION QUALIFICATION

The installation qualification section of this protocol will verify that all components are installed as specified: critical drawings reflect the current status of the system; critical manuals concerning operation and maintenance are available and utilities necessary for operation are properly installed.

2.1   Document all the designated personnel assigned the responsibility of executing or verifying the execution of this protocol. Record this information on IQ-A.

2.2   Document all critical manuals necessary for operation and maintenance. Record information on IQ-B.

2.3   Document all critical drawings of system components necessary for operation and maintenance. Record information on IQ-C.

2.4   Document required utilities necessary for operation are installed correctly. Record information on IQ-D.

2.5   Document all Materials of Construction (MOC) of product contact surfaces (not recorded elsewhere). Record information on IQ-E.

	Title: Shelf Dryer System IO/PQ Protocol
	Document #: XXX-XX-X_XXXXX
	Revision Date:
	Page 7 of 38

3.0 OPERATIONAL QUALIFICATION

The Operational Qualification section of this Protocol will address two issues.

3.1 Critical Documentation

Critical documentation associated with the operation of this system will be documented on the appropriate sheet. This will include standard operating procedures, preventative maintenance work orders, training documents, critical & non-critical instruments, validation test instruments and calibration records for all instruments.

3.1.1 Document all current and needed SOP's. Record information on OQ-A.

3.1.2 Document all preventative maintenance work orders, record information on OQ-B. Review the current PM's and verify they address all critical aspects of the system. Attach copies of PM's to the Summary Report.

3.1.3 Verify training documentation is in place for system users. Include individual/department responsible for maintenance of such records. Record information on OQ-C. Attach copies of sample training records to the Summary Report.

3.1.4 Document all instruments associated with the system that are on a calibration schedule on OQ-D. Attach copies of the calibration documents to the Summary Report.

3.1.5 Document all instruments used for testing during the Protocol execution. Record information on OQ-E. Attach copies of calibration documentation to the Summary Report.

Reviewed By: _____ . Date: _____

	Title: Shelf Dryer System IO/PQ Protocol
	Document #: XXX-XX-X_XXXXX
	Revision Date:
	Page 8 of 38

3.2 Functional Testing

Critical functions will be tested to verify they operate as designed. The test procedure will be identified on the appropriate sheet, along with the test results.

3.2.1 Verify all alarms on the Shelf Dryer System. See Test Sheet #1.

3.2.2 Verify Out of Range Data Entry. See Test Sheet #2.

3.2.3 Verify True Data Entry. See Test Sheet #3.

3.2.4 Verify the rotation of the re-circulating pump motor. See Test Sheet #4.

Verify all standard operating functions. See Test Sheet #4

4.0 PERFORMANCE QUALIFICATION

The following Performance Test will verify and document that the Shelf Dryer System (XX) operates in a manner consistent with the applicable specifications.

The Performance Test is the process that tests critical attributes of the system via the test cases contained in this section.

For the tests contained in this Performance Test section, the person executing the test cases must survey the equipment/system listed in the installed position and observe the critical attributes listed. The test procedure will be identified on the appropriate sheet, along with the test results.

4.1 Temperature Distribution Study

Execute and verify Temperature Distribution Study. See Test Sheet #6

5.0 GENERAL INFORMATION

In each Test Sheet there is a comment section that must be filled out if any anomaly occurs during the test. The anomaly and the reason for the anomaly will be explained and the actions taken.

Reviewed By: _____ . Date:_____

	Title: Shelf Dryer System IO/PQ Protocol
	Document #: XXX-XX-X_XXXXX
	Revision Date:
	Page 9 of 38

Actual results of the Protocol will be documented by the use of either Y/N entries, printed outputs, and/or tester data entries as indicated by the test. Y/N entries indicate the actual results have been observed as detailed by the expected results.

6.0 SUMMARY REPORT

A Summary Report of the tests and results will be issued following the Protocol execution. Qualification and test results will be addressed along with any noted anomalies. The conclusion statement will address the validation status of the system.

IQ – A – SIGNATURE VERIFICATION FORM

Designated personnel assigned the responsibility of executing or verifying execution of this protocol must sign, initial and date the table below.				
Print Name	Signature	Initials	Department	Date

Comments

Reviewed By: _____. Date:_____

	Title: Shelf Dryer System IO/PQ Protocol
	Document #: XXX-XX-X_XXXXX
	Revision Date:
	Page 10 of 38

IQ – B – CRITICAL MANUAL DOCUMENTATION

The following manual(s) has/have been identified as critical.		
Manual / Document Title	**Library Number**	**Location**

Are additional manuals needed for this system?   **Error! Reference source not found.**☐ **Error! Reference source not found.** Yes   ☐**Error! Reference source not found. Error! Reference source not found.** No

If "Yes", continue list on reverse side of this page.

Comments

Reviewed By: _____. Date:_____

	Title: Shelf Dryer System IO/PQ Protocol
	Document #: XXX-XX-X_XXXXX
	Revision Date:
	Page 11 of 38

IQ – C – DRAWING VERIFICATION

Drawing Title	Drawing Number	Revision	Location	Drawing Reflects Current Status of System (Yes/No)?

Comments

Reviewed By:_____. Date_____

	Title: Shelf Dryer System IO/PQ Protocol
	Document #: XXX-XX-X_XXXXX
	Revision Date:
	Page 12 of 38

IQ – D – UTILITY DOCUMENTATION
(Page 1 of 2)

ELECTRICAL SUPPLY

Using the appropriate calibrated test instrument(s), measure the utilities as per the table below. Follow appropriate safety procedures including use of qualified specialist.

Service	(**) As Specified	As Supplied	Supply Meets Requirement (Y/N)?	System Connected to Emergency Power (Y/N)?	Performed By (Initials/Date)
Control Panel					
AC Voltage					
Phase					
Amperage					
TCU					
AC Voltage					
Phase					
Amperage					

Emergency Power		
Service	Installed (Yes/No)	Performed By (Initials/Date)
Emergency Power		

Reviewed By:_____. Date_____

	Title: Shelf Dryer System IO/PQ Protocol
	Document #: XXX-XX-X_XXXXX
	Revision Date:
	Page 13 of 38

IQ – D – UTILITY DOCUMENTATION
(Page 2 of 2)

Utility	As Specified		As Found		Performed By (Initials/Date)
	Line Size	Service Requirements	Line Size	Service Requirements	
Nitrogen					
Process Water					
CHWS Supply					
CHWR Return					
Vent Header					
Vacuum					

(**) As Specified = specifications by manufacturer or as required per operation as specified in the batch (or equivalent) records.

Comments

Reviewed By: _____ Date: _____

	Title: Shelf Dryer System IO/PQ Protocol
	Document #: XXX-XX-X_XXXXX
	Revision Date:
	Page 14 of 38

IQ – E – MATERIALS OF CONSTRUCTION (MOC) OF PRODUCT CONTACT SURFACES

Component	MOC	Performed By (Initials/Date)

Comments

Reviewed By: _____ Date: _____

	Title: Shelf Dryer System (D-23) IO/PQ Protocol
	Document #: XXX-XX-X_XXXXX
	Revision Date:
	Page 15 of 38

OQ – A – STANDARD OPERATING PROCEDURES

Title	SOP Number	Effective Date	Location

Do current SOP's address critical issues? ☐ Yes ☐ No
Are Additional SOP's Required? ☐ Yes ☐ No
If "Yes", continue list on reverse side of this page.

OQ – B – PREVENTATIVE MAINTENANCE WORK ORDERS

Title	Reference Number	Work Order Adequate / Complete (Y/N)

OQ – C – TRAINING DOCUMENTATION

Training Documentation	Location	Individual / Department Responsible

Comments

Performed By: _____ Date: _____

Reviewed By: _____ Date: _____

	Title: Shelf Dryer System (D-23) IO/PQ Protocol
	Document #: XXX-XX-X_XXXXX
	Revision Date:
	Page 16 of 38

OQ – D – CRITICAL INSTRUMENT INVENTORY

I.D. Number	Description	Parameter	Last Cal. Date	Next Cal. Date
	List all critical instruments associated with the system on a calibration schedule.			
	Process Water Make-Up Pressure Regulator	Pressure		
	Temperature Transmitter and RTD.	Temperature		
	Temperature Control Unit	Temperature		
	Nitrogen Pressure Regulator	Pressure		
	Vacuum Line Pressure Transmitter (PIT-06)	Pressure		
	CHWS flow meter (FI-20)	Flow		
	Circulation Pump Supply Pressure Indicator	Pressure		
	Circulation Pump Return Pressure Indicator	Pressure		
	CHWR Temperature Indicator	Temperature		
	Electric Heater Outlet Temperature Indicator	Temperature		
	Electric Heater Outlet Pressure Indicator	Pressure		
	Nitrogen Flow Indicator	Flow		
	Nitrogen Pressure Indicator	Pressure		
	Vacuum Line Pressure Indicator	Pressure		
	Vacuum Line Pressure Indicator	Pressure		

* Indicates instrument on a calibration schedule

Comments

Performed By: _____ Date: _____

Reviewed By: _____ Date: _____

	Title: Shelf Dryer System (D-23) IO/PQ Protocol
	Document #: XXX-XX-X_XXXXX
	Revision Date:
	Page 17 of 38

OQ – E – TEST INSTRUMENT DOCUMENTATION

List all instruments used for testing during this validation.

Inventory Number	Description	Parameter	Pre Cal. Date	Post Cal. Date

* Indicates instrument on a calibration schedule

Comments

Performed By: _____ Date: _____

Reviewed By: _____ Date: _____

	Title: Shelf Dryer System (D-23) IO/PQ Protocol
	Document #: XXX-XX-X_XXXXX
	Revision Date:
	Page 18 of 38

TEST SHEET #1 - ALARM SIGNAL VERIFICATION
(Page 1 of 2)

Objective:

To confirm that the alarms provide the expected alarm level response.

Procedure:

1. Verify all alarms and their proper response by triggering the field devices, where possible, and simulating an alarm input, as necessary. One of the following verification procedures will be employed for each alarm verification:

   A1   Change the set point
   A2   Trigger the alarm condition at the field device
   A3   Manipulate the software utility to manipulate the I/O's
   A4   Simulate alarm with voltage/current simulator or software utility
   A5   Method other than above

2. Record which of the five methods was used to activate and verify an alarm by writing it in the "Activation Method" column. If method "A5" is used, explain in the comments area the method used to trigger the alarm.

3. If the alarm message displayed matches the "Alarm Description", write "Y" for yes in the "Alarm Message As Expected" column. Write "N" for no if it does not.

4. Repeat above steps for each alarm listed.

Acceptance Criteria:

The alarms provide the expected alarm level response

	Title: Shelf Dryer System (D-23) IO/PQ Protocol
	Document #: XXX-XX-X_XXXXX
	Revision Date:
	Page 19 of 38

TEST SHEET #1 - ALARM SIGNAL VERIFICATION
(Page 2 of 2)

Alarm	Description	Method of Verification	Alarm message as expected (Y/N)	Alarm Reset (Y/N)	Performed By Initials/Date
Low Jacket Temperature Alarm					
High Jacket Temperature Alarm					
Low Chamber Pressure Alarm					
High Chamber Pressure Alarm					

Comments

Reviewed By: _____ _____ Date: _____

	Title: Shelf Dryer System (D-23) IO/PQ Protocol
	Document #: XXX-XX-X_XXXXX
	Revision Date:
	Page 20 of 38

TEST SHEET #2 – OUT OF RANGE ENTRY DATA TEST
(Page 1 of 2)

Objective:

To verify that the system will not accept parameter values outside the specified range.

Procedure:

For "Out of Range" data enter and record values that are above and below the given range of each parameter. Enter values one unit above and below the entry range. If the system rejects a value entered, write "Y" for yes in the appropriate "System Rejects Value" column or "N" for no if it accepts it. Initial and date the "Performed By" column.

Acceptance Criteria:

All out of range data and all non entered parameters, outside of the specified range, are rejected and not accepted by the system.

	Title: Shelf Dryer System (D-23) IO/PQ Protocol
	Document #: XXX-XX-X_XXXXX
	Revision
	Page 21 of 38

TEST SHEET #2 – OUT OF RANGE ENTRY DATA TEST
(Page 2 of 2)

Parameter	Data Entry Range	Value Below Min. Data Entry Range	System Rejects Value (Y/N)?	Value Above Max. Data Entry Range	System Rejects Value (Y/N)?	Performed By (Initial/Date)
TCU shelf temperature control set point.						
Chamber pressure control set point.						

Comments

Performed By: _____ Date: _____

Reviewed By: _____ Date: _____

	Title: Shelf Dryer System (D-23) IO/PQ Protocol
	Document #: XXX-XX-X_XXXXX
	Revision Date:
	Page 22 of 38

TEST SHEET #3 – TRUE DATA ENTRY TEST

(Page 1 of 2)

Objective:

To verify that the system will accept only parameter values within the specified range.

Procedure:

For "True" data enter the minimum and maximum values provided in the table for each parameter as well as a value between the minimum and maximum values. If the system accepts an entered value write "Y" for yes in the "System Accepts Value" column or "N" for no if it does not accept it. Initial and date the "Performed By" column.

Acceptance Criteria:

All true data parameters, within the specified range, are accepted by the system.

	Title: Shelf Dryer System (D-23) IO/PQ Protocol
	Document #: XXX-XX-X_XXXXX
	Revision Date:
	Page 23 of 38

TEST SHEET #3 – TRUE DATA ENTRY TEST
(Page 2 of 3)

Parameter	Value At Min. Data Entry Range	System Accepts Value (Y/N)?	Value At Max. Data Entry Range	System Accepts Value (Y/N)?	Value In Acceptable Data Range	System Accepts Value (Y/N)?	Performed By (Initial/Date)
TCU shelf temperature control set point.							
Chamber pressure control set point.							

Comments

Performed By: _____ Date: _____

Reviewed By: _____ Date: _____

	Title: Shelf Dryer System (D-23) IO/PQ Protocol
	Document #: XXX-XX-X_XXXXX
	Revision Date:

TEST SHEET #4 – CIRCULATION PUMP MOTOR ROTATION TEST

Test Objective:

To verify that the Circulation Pump Motor rotates in the proper direction.

Test Procedure:

Visually observe the following and compare with the expected results as outlined in the data table:

1. Start up the Shelf Dryer System (XX) according to the operating instructions. Verify that the circulation pump motor rotates in the correct direction through visual inspection.
2. Shut down the Shelf Dryer System (XX) according to the operating instructions.

Acceptance Criteria:

Circulation Pump Motor rotates in the proper direction..

PUMP MOTOR ROTATION TEST			
Motor Description	**Expected Direction**	**Actual Direction**	**Performed By (Init./Date)**
Circulation Pump Motor			

Comments

Reviewed By: _____ Date_____

	Title: Shelf Dryer System (D-23) IO/PQ Protocol
	Document #: XXX-XX-X_XXXXX
	Revision Date:

TEST SHEET #5 – FUNCTIONAL VERIFICATION
(Page 1 of 3)

Test Objective:

Verify all controls and adjustments will produce the expected results.

Procedure:

Execute the steps as indicated in table. In the "Actual Results match Expected" column record a Y if the results match the Expected Results or an N if they do not.

Acceptance Criteria:

All entries into the "Actual Results as Expected" column will be "Y

Reviewed By: _____   Date_____

	Title: Shelf Dryer System (D-23) IO/PQ Protocol
	Document #: XXX-XX-X_XXXXX
	Revision Date:
	Page 26 of 38

TEST SHEET #5 – FUNCTIONAL VERIFICATION
(Page 2 of 3)

Function	Test	Expected Result	Actual Results Match Expected (Y/N)	Performed By Initial/Date
Circulation Pump	Following operating procedures start the circulation pump.			
TCU	Set temperature controller to the 'Auto' position			
	Set XXX-XXX-x to the 'Cool' position			
	Set temperature controller setpoint to xxx			
	Set temperature controller setpoint to xx°C.			
Chamber Pressure Control	Set pressure controller to +XXX.			
	Set pressure controller to -XXX.			

Performed By: _____ Date: _____

Reviewed By: _____ Date: _____

	Title: Shelf Dryer System (D-23) VIO/PQ Protocol
	Document #: XXX-XX-X_XXXXX
	Revision Date:
	Page 27 of 38

TEST SHEET #5 – FUNCTIONAL VERIFICATION
(Page 3 of 3)

Comments

Performed By: _____ Date: _____

Reviewed By: _____ Date: _____

	Title: Shelf Dryer System (D-23) IO/PQ Protocol
	Document #: XXX-XX-X_XXXXX
	Revision Date:
	Page 28 of 38

TEST SHEET #6 – TEMPERATURE DISTRIBUTION STUDY
(Page 1 of 10)

Test Objective:

The Shelf Dryer System (XX) must be able to bring materials to and maintain them at required temperatures. This test is performed to verify that the Shelf Dryer System (XX) is able to maintain the required chamber temperature over an extended period of time.

Procedure:

(1)   Monitor the temperature at multiple points inside the Shelf Dryer System (XX) for a 48 hour period.

(2)   This temperature distribution study will performed at five (5) different temperature control setpoints. First it will be executed at xx°C, then at yyC, followed by zz°C, aaC and then ss°C (execute them in this order).

(3)   Following xxx procedures, a Pre-Calibration and a Post-Calibration will be performed on the temperature sensors that will be used for this Temperature Distribution Study. The temperature sensors and the reference must agree to within ± 0.5°C and demonstrate a stability of ≤ 0.2°C for a minimum of five (5) minutes. Attach a copy of the calibration reports.

(4)   The temperature sensors should be placed four (4) to six (6) inches from walls and other objects other than shelves that product will be placed on.

(5)   The temperature sensors should be placed in two planes and one (1) next to or in close proximity to the chamber control probe. Plane 1 should be placed on Shelf #1. Plane 2 should be placed on Shelf #2. Five (5) temperature sensors will be placed on each of the two (2) shelves. Label the temperature sensors according to "Temperature Sensor Location Table".

(6)   Two additional temperature sensors will be used for informational data only. One will be placed on the heating/cooling medium inlet piping leading to the dryer chamber, and the second one will be placed on the heating/cooling medium outlet piping leading from the dryer chamber. These sensors will not be averaged in to readings from the sensors that are placed inside the chamber. Label these temperature sensors according to "Temperature Sensor Location Table".

(7)   Program the data acquisition instrument to record the temperature of each temperature sensor at ten (10) minute intervals

	Title: Shelf Dryer System (D-23) IO/PQ Protocol
	Document #: XXX-XX-X_XXXXX
	Revision Date:
	Page 29 of 38

TEST SHEET #6 – TEMPERATURE DISTRIBUTION STUDY
(Page 2 of 10)

(8)   Initiate the temperature data acquisition instrument to record temperature for a minimum of forty eight (48) continuous hours after the Shelf Dryer System (XX) chamber reaches temperature.

TEMPERATURE SENSOR LOCATION TABLE	
SENSOR NO.	**LOCATION**
1A	Shelf 1, Position 1a.
1B	Shelf 1, Position 1b.
1C	Shelf 1, Position 1c.
1D	Shelf 1, Position 1d.
1E	Shelf 1, Position 1e.
2A	Shelf 1, Position 2a.
2B	Shelf 1, Position 2b.
2C	Shelf 1, Position 2c.
2D	Shelf 1, Position 2d.
2E	Shelf 1, Position 2e.
3	Position 3, Next to the chamber control/monitoring probe.
4	Position 4, Chamber heating/cooling medium inlet.
5	Position 5, Chamber heating/cooling medium outlet.

Performed By: _____ Date: _____

Reviewed By: _____ Date: _____

	Title: Shelf Dryer System (D-23) IO/PQ Protocol
	Document #: XXX-XX-X_XXXXX
	Revision Date:
	Page 30 of 38

TEST SHEET #6 – TEMPERATURE DISTRIBUTION STUDY
(Page 3 of 10)
TEMPERATURE SENSOR LOCATION DIAGRAM

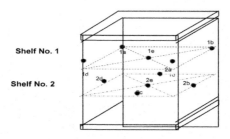

Position 3 is next to the chamber control/monitoring probe.
Position 4 is on the chamber heating/cooling medium inlet.
Position 5 is on the chamber heating/cooling medium outlet.

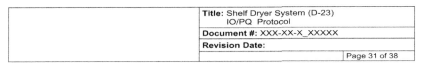

	Title: Shelf Dryer System (D-23) IO/PQ Protocol
	Document #: XXX-XX-X_XXXXX
	Revision Date:
	Page 31 of 38

TEST SHEET #6 – TEMPERATURE DISTRIBUTION STUDY
(Page 4 of 10)

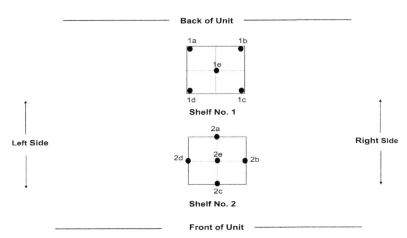

Position 3 is next to the chamber control/monitoring probe.
Position 4 is on the chamber heating/cooling medium inlet.
Position 5 is on the chamber heating/cooling medium outlet.

	Title: Shelf Dryer System (D-23) IO/PQ Protocol
	Document #: XXX-XX-X_XXXXX
	Revision Date:
	Page 32 of 38

TEST SHEET #6 – TEMPERATURE DISTRIBUTION STUDY
(Page 5 of 10)

Acceptance Criteria:

(1)   All temperature sensors must remain within ±1°C of the temperature control setpoint during the temperature exposure period for each of the forty-eight hour runs.

(2)   The coldest and warmest points of the Shelf Dryer System (XX) should be identified and documented.

(3)   The results of the distribution study agree with the trend on the chart recorder.

(4)   The Shelf Dryer System (XX) is able to bring materials up to or down to and maintain them at required temperatures.

(5)   The Shelf Dryer System (XX) is able to maintain the required chamber temperature over an extended period of time.

	Title: Shelf Dryer System (D-23) IO/PQ Protocol
	Document #: XXX-XX-X_XXXXX
	Revision Date:
	Page 33 of 38

TEST SHEET #6 – TEMPERATURE DISTRIBUTION STUDY
(Page 6 of 10)

RESULTS SUMMARY (80°C)			
Date Initiated: _____		Time Initiated: _____	
Date Ended: _____		Time Ended: _____	

DESCRIPTION	SENSOR NUMBER	TEMPERATURE (°C)	PERFORMED BY (INITIAL/DATE)
Maximum Recorded Temperature			
Minimum Recorded Temperature			
Maximum Average Temperature (Hottest Spot)			
Minimum Average Temperature (Coldest Spot)			

Comments

Performed By: _____ Date: _____

Reviewed By: _____ Date: _____

	Title: Shelf Dryer System (D-23) IO/PQ Protocol
	Document #: XXX-XX-X_XXXXX
	Revision Date:
	Page 34 of 38

TEST SHEET #6 – TEMPERATURE DISTRIBUTION STUDY
(Page 7 of 10)

RESULTS SUMMARY (95°C)			
Date Initiated: _____		Time Initiated: _____	
Date Ended: _____		Time Ended: _____	
DESCRIPTION	**SENSOR NUMBER**	**TEMPERATURE (°C)**	**PERFORMED BY (INITIAL/DATE)**
Maximum Recorded Temperature			
Minimum Recorded Temperature			
Maximum Average Temperature (Hottest Spot)			
Minimum Average Temperature (Coldest Spot)			

Comments

Performed By: _____ Date: _____

Reviewed By: _____ Date: _____

	Title: Shelf Dryer System (D-23) IO/PQ Protocol
	Document #: XXX-XX-X_XXXXX
	Revision Date:
	Page 35 of 38

TEST SHEET #6 – TEMPERATURE DISTRIBUTION STUDY
(Page 8 of 10)

RESULTS SUMMARY (60°C)			
Date Initiated: _____		Time Initiated: _____	
Date Ended: _____		Time Ended: _____	
DESCRIPTION	SENSOR NUMBER	TEMPERATURE (°C)	PERFORMED BY (INITIAL/DATE)
Maximum Recorded Temperature			
Minimum Recorded Temperature			
Maximum Average Temperature (Hottest Spot)			
Minimum Average Temperature (Coldest Spot)			

Comments

Performed By: _____ Date: _____

Reviewed By: _____ Date: _____

	Title: Shelf Dryer System (D-23) IO/PQ Protocol
	Document #: XXX-XX-X_XXXXX
	Revision Date:
	Page 36 of 38

TEST SHEET #6 – TEMPERATURE DISTRIBUTION STUDY
(Page 9 of 10)

RESULTS SUMMARY (20°C)			
Date Initiated: _____		Time Initiated: _____	
Date Ended: _____		Time Ended: _____	
DESCRIPTION	**SENSOR NUMBER**	**TEMPERATURE (°C)**	**PERFORMED BY (INITIAL/DATE)**
Maximum Recorded Temperature			
Minimum Recorded Temperature			
Maximum Average Temperature (Hottest Spot)			
Minimum Average Temperature (Coldest Spot)			

Comments

Performed By: _____ Date: _____

Reviewed By: _____ Date: _____

	Title: Shelf Dryer System (D-23) IO/PQ Protocol
	Document #: XXX-XX-X_XXXXX
	Revision Date:
	Page 37 of 38

TEST SHEET #6 – TEMPERATURE DISTRIBUTION STUDY
(Page 10 of 10)

RESULTS SUMMARY (40°C)			
Date Initiated: _____		Time Initiated: _____	
Date Ended: _____		Time Ended: _____	
DESCRIPTION	**SENSOR NUMBER**	**TEMPERATURE (°C)**	**PERFORMED BY (INITIAL/DATE)**
Maximum Recorded Temperature			
Minimum Recorded Temperature			
Maximum Average Temperature (Hottest Spot)			
Minimum Average Temperature (Coldest Spot)			

Comments

Performed By: _____ Date: _____

Reviewed By: _____ Date: _____

	Title: Shelf Dryer System (D-23) IO/PQ Protocol
	Document #: XXX-XX-X_XXXXX
	Revision Date:
	Page 38 of 38

7.0 POST APPROVAL

PROTOCOL REVIEWED BY: _____ DATE: _____
                      Name
                      Print _____
                      Company

APPROVED BY: _____ DATE: _____
             Name
             Print _____
             Company

Engineering _____ DATE: _____
            Name
            Print _____
            Company

R & D_ _____ DATE: _____
       Name
       Print _____
       Company

QA. _____ DATE: _____
    Name
    Print _____
    Company

Performed By: _____ Date: _____

Reviewed By: _____ Date: _____

Sample IQ/OQ Protocol Final Report

Scope

 This report finalizes the IQ and OQ testing for XXXXXX. The IQ and OQ covered the major physical components of the unit as well as its functionality according to both the manufacturer and COMPANY located in City, State.

Conclusion

 This unit has been tested in its IQ and OQ functionality and has been shown to meet all requirement necessary for use in production. As seen in the tables all major components are labeled and all components necessary for its operation according to the needs of the COMPANY and the process are present. The OQ tests listed in Table Z demonstrate that the unit is fully operational across its operational range as specified by the manufacturer.

Results

 Table(s)

Discussion

 How the test were run and a discussion of the results

Deviations

 List all deviations and the remediation steps taken to resolve them

References

Regulations—FDA (www.fda.gov or www.gpo.gov)

1. 21 CFR Part 11—Electronic Records and Signatures
2. 21 CFR Part 210—GMP
3. 21 CFR Part 211—GMP
4. 21 CFR Part 600—Biological/Blood
5. 21 CFR Part 820—QSR Devices

FDA Guidelines https://www.fda.gov/ForIndustry/Industry NoticesandGuidanceDocuments/default.htm

1. Process analytical technology (PAT)
2. Guide to inspections validation of cleaning processes
3. Quality Systems Inspection Technique (QSIT)
4. GMPs for the 21st Century
5. Sterile Drug Products Produced by Aseptic Processing—Current Good Manufacturing Practice
6. Process Validation—2011

ICH Guidelines

1. Q 8—Pharmaceutical development
2. Q 9—Risk management
3. Q 10—Quality systems

Books

1. Pharmaceutical Process Scale Up—Ed., M. Levin; Informa Healthcare.
2. Validation of Pharmaceutical Processes, Ed., J. Agalloco & F. Carlton; Informa Healthcare, 3rd Ed., 2007, Chapters 9 & 47.
3. Good Manufacturing Practices for Pharmaceuticals—Ed., J. Nalley; Informa Healthcare.
4. ISPE Baseline Guides #1–6.
5. Validation of Pharmaceutical Processes, Ed. R. Nash & A. Wachter, 2003, Marcel Decker.
6. Application of Pharmaceutical GMPs – D. Barr, et. Al.; FDLI.
7. Validation Fundamentals—W. Gibson, K. Powell-Evans; Interpharm/CRC.
8. Statistical Solutions; L. Torbeck; Pharm Tech, 10/2009.
9. PDA Technical Reports—(TR 60, TR 60.2, & TR 18).
10. Pharmaceutical Operations Management, P. Mohan, J. Glassey, & G. Montague, McGraw Hill, 2006.

Other

1. https://learnaboutgmp.com/good-validation-practices/defining-calibration-qualification-of-equipment/.

2. https://www.softwaretestinghelp.com/iq-oq-pq-software-validation/.

3. https://www.nist.gov/calibrations/recommended calibration-interval.

4. FREQUENCY OF CALIBRATION: A CRITICAL ISSUE FOR QUALITY CONTROL IN THE PHARMACEUTICAL INDUSTRY *Willians Portella and Maurício N. Frota* XVIII IMEKO WORLD CONGRESS Metrology for a Sustainable Development September, 17–22, 2006, Rio de Janeiro, Brazil.

5. https://learnaboutgmp.com/good-validation-practices/defining-calibration-qualification-of-equipment/.

6. Preventive maintenance strategies for the pharmaceutical industry. An overview of the issues to consider when implementing a preventative maintenance strategy. Wayne Collins Pharmaceutical Technology Europe Nov 01, 2007,Volume 19, Issue 11.

7. VALIDATION, QUALIFICATION AND CALIBRATION IN A PHARMACEUTICAL FACILITY, LAB SERVICES NEWS | QUALITY CONTROL TESTING, February 12, 2014, Marco Benvenuti, Business Manager Life Science Italy, SGS Life Science Services, SGS Sertec, Livorno, Italy.

8. https://www.fda.gov/downloads/drugs/developmentapprovalprocess/smallbusinessassistance/ucm456370.pdf.

9. http://www.ivtnetwork.com/article/writing-pharmaceutical-equipment-qualification-protocols.

10. https://www.getreskilled.com/what-are-iq-oq-pq/.

Index

Note: Page numbers followed by *f* indicate figures and *t* indicate tables.

Printed in the United States
By Bookmasters